To Jill.

A wonderf...

by a frie...

Roken.

THEY STOLE MY PARENTS

Also by the same author:

PARASITES AND PARASITISM

GARDEN OF THE DEEP

ECOLOGY OF A CAVE

BEFORE NATURE DIED

THEY STOLE MY PARENTS

LIA CRUICKSHANK

Sylvana Books

First Published 1993
by Sylvana Books,
23, Melton Way,
Shrewsbury.

British Library
Cataloguing-in-Publication
Data

ISBN 0-9522635-0-5

Printed by Cambrian Printers, Aberystwyth.

Lia Cruickshank is a Doctor of Biology who was an editor for nineteen years at the Scientific Publishing House in Bucharest. Normally she writes scientific books in her speciality, but this time she has taken the opportunity to tell the dramatic story of her early life.

She now lives with her husband in the beautiful Shropshire countryside where she writes, translates and enjoys a peaceful life.

With thanks to my husband, William, for his help and encouragement in writing this book.

Also to Molly Hazzard for her corrections and helpful criticism.

In Memory of *Mama* and *Tata*

INTRODUCTION

In the South of Russia, on the border with Romania, lies the small Republic of Moldavia, known in the past as Bessarabia. This strip of land between the rivers Prut and Dnistru, abounding in low hills, woodland, fertile agricultural land, vineyards and orchards, is my homeland.

The region has had a very troubled past, being disputed, fought over and invaded many times by Poles, Greeks, Bulgars, Turks and Russians. In 1859 Bessarabia became part of the newly founded country of Romania, but not for long, as in 1878 Russia annexed this region as a protectorate and it stayed so until the first World War, after which it was returned to Romania as part of the peace agreements.

However, between the two World Wars this agreement was constantly disputed by Russia, who regarded Bessarabia as hers in spite of the fact that the inhabitants look upon themselves as Romanian and speak that language.

I was born in 1932 in the central part of Bessarabia, not far from Orhei, in the small village of Slobozia, when the region belonged to Romania. At the time my story begins, in 1936, the political situation of Romania was far from stable. King Carol, who ruled the country, involved himself in a great deal of intrigue, firstly supporting a fascist group called the Iron Guard, then turning against this organisation after it had assassinated the prime minister. He even declared himself dictator. When Russia threatened to occupy Bessarabia and Hungary, Transylvania, Carol appealed to Hitler for help. The Fuhrer promised aid, but in 1939 Ribbentrop and Molotov made a secret treaty that Bessarabia would go once again to Russia, and one year later Hitler, reneging on his promise of help, forced Carol to hand Bessarabia to Stalin.

In 1941, when the German troops attacked Russia, the region was liberated, but only for a short time, because in 1944, as the Germans retreated, Russia once again occupied Bessarabia. By now Carol had abdicated and his son, King Michael, pulled Romania out of the war. After the occupation Bessarabia was called the Soviet Republic of Moldavia and it has stayed under the iron grip of Russia until recent years, when the region began the struggle to become independent.

ONE

The old white house covered in rough thatch, the wonder of the deep blue sky of hot summer days, the fascination of the brightly coloured fluttering butterflies, and the soaring swooping flight of swallows are the earliest memories I have as I look back into that time, decades ago, as into a painting by Degas or Renoir. I discover myself, a little four year old, clad in a sleeveless plain blue dress, bare footed, in the yard of my parent's farm, situated at one end of the village of Slobozia. Looking across the vegetable garden, separated from a huge green meadow by the watery barrier of a small river, I can see the field rising in a gentle slope to become a low hill, gashed like a great open mouth by the yellow cleft from which the villagers dug clay to make bricks for their houses.

At this time the boundaries of my world were very definite. They were marked all around me by the place where the blue sky was stitched along the hem of the green and brown land. Within this scope was all that I knew. The farm, the houses within my vision, the fields, insects, birds and my family. That the real world extended far beyond had never occurred to me, and therefore never excited my imagination.

In this farmyard, the very hub of my world and my existence, there was so much to see, so many places to explore, so much life bustling about me. I was looked after with loving care by my large family: *Mama* and *Tata*, my half brothers George and Ephraim, my brothers John, Constantin and Basil, and my sisters Mary and Sanda (short for Alexandra).

My father had been married once before to Maria, who died in childbirth at the coming of their second son. Left with two young children, George and Ephraim, he was obliged to remarry before long. He was only twenty seven, considered handsome, with some property, and there were many girls in the village and the countryside who were waiting to be asked in marriage.

From all of them he chose Nicola, then twenty two, who came from a respectable family. The marriage was an excuse for a big celebration, after which Nicola moved into the Slobozia house to become the instant mother of the two little boys.

Before very long she began to have her own children. First John, then three years later, Constantin, followed after a similar interval by Basil. By then she was rather tired of boys, having by now five to look after. Finally the stork brought her a girl, Mary.

"What a great joy that was for me, the first girl, with the promise that in the future I would have someone to help me in the house!" *Mama* exclaimed once. Then came myself and after two years, Sanda. We were both rather an anti climax, I imagine, as all the excitement had been for the first girl.

When my story starts, in 1936, we were seven children in the yard, the eighth, George, being already married at eighteen and living with his in-laws.

As far as my brothers were concerned Mary, Sanda and I, when little, constituted a burden they had to bear. *Mama*, always busy, decided on sharing responsibility at an early age and appointed each brother to have a sister as his special charge. I was put in the care of Constantin. His main duty, when I was a baby, was to rock the cradle, made from a section of hollowed out tree trunk, suspended on ropes hung from the ceiling beams. Itching to get outside, where the others were playing, he would rock me back and forth every frustrated minute, glaring intently until my eyes closed, which he took as his signal for release, but many a time, before he had managed to open the door, I began to wail. To his utter chagrin he had to return again to the boring rocking, enduring the torture of hearing his brothers enjoying themselves in the sunshine outdoors.

There were two houses on our farm, one old and one more recently built. We lived mostly in the older house which for some reason was much warmer in winter and it had a larger kitchen which Mum preferred to use. The new house had larger windows and in some ways was more attractive than the old one, but it was mainly used when we had guests or family gatherings or on special days. Although for me the whole farm was my domain, my world and my paradise, it was the older house which gave me the greatest feeling of warmth, love and life. I suppose this white house must have been quite crowded at the time with so many of us even after George married Marika and moved out, but if so it never raised a thought in my young head.

On one side of this old house, behind two doors, many steps led down to a vast cellar, full of barrels and boxes, jars and bottles and a multitude of scents and odours and sometimes the scurrying of tiny feet. To me it was rather dark and frightening. I much preferred to be on the wide wooden verandah, clothed in a curtain of vines, whose large green leaves formed such a lovely cool barrier against the heat of the summer sun.

Behind the new house extended a large fruit orchard of apples, pears, quinces and plums and, largest of all, the giant walnut trees. Between these trees, each spring, Dad placed his beehives, taken from their winter shelter in one of the barns. Some of the hives were quite old, being fashioned from hollow tree trunk sections, into which specially shaped combs fitted. On their tops sat large conical lids of baked clay, looking to me like giant Chinese hatted mushrooms.

Dad loved the bees, which were truly his pets, fussed over and cared for. I saw him often near the hives, head covered in an old straw hat, with a net hanging down to his shoulders like a dirty veil, sleeves tied tightly about the wrists.

There was a path through the fruit trees ending at a wattle fence, pierced by a gate of the same twisted branches. This separated us from our next door neighbour, whom I knew as Auntie Mary, but it was a gate I feared to go too near, for on the other side there also lived a huge gangling hound, whose ferocious bark would roar out if someone approached his territory. I knew he was kept on a chain, but I was not brave enough to believe that he could not get to me if I dared to go close to his kingdom. There were also the bees to contend with. They buzzed past me in a constant stream back and fourth to the hives and if I waved them away they would only get noisier and buzz nearer. But they never did sting me and I soon came to realize that if I ignored them they would do the same to me.

Sheds and stables led away at right angles from the house, serving as shelters for the horses and as a store, in which large wooden bins with hinged lids contained the reserves of cereals and flour. One barn, with doors so wide and high that a load of hay could be driven through, housed the carts and sledge. Another held the saddles and bridles, the agricultural tools and the plough. Last of all, but most important, was the tall thin wattle construction in which Dad stored the heads of maize. There was a loft over part of the stables building and in this were kept the baskets of walnuts, sacks of dried peas and beans and the long ropes of garlic and onions. There were dozens of delightful places in which to play hide-and-seek.

During the weekdays everyone in the family except Mum, Sanda and myself were either out working in the fields, or at school. Too young to do anything about the house, I was supposed to look after my little sister while Mum worked. Sanda, however, was quite content playing, sometimes completely nude, with the nearest patch of mud, her dress, which she had wriggled out of, lying somewhere about in the yard. Mum did not seem to mind Sanda getting dirty. She usually picked her up, mud covered, carried her to the well and washed her, saying, "Come, my mucky little angel, I'll clean you up once again". It was a waste of effort, for by the time Mum had reached the house Sanda had either fallen over or found some fresh goo to play with. As she was the only blonde in the family, and the youngest, everyone spoiled her a little.

Althought I thought it fun rescuing Sanda from her muddy adventures each day I always looked forward eagerly to the end of school, when my brothers and Mary returned home and brought action and excitement to the yard.

Usually the gate crashed open and John and Constantin burst through, often arguing but always inseparable. They were such different characters, John cocky, self assured, to whom everything was a laugh or joke except his clothes and his appearance, which were serious matters. Clean, neat and fastidious, he was fussy about anything he wore, constantly straightening his tunic. Constantin, on the other hand, couldn't have cared less about his dress. He would arrive with shirt hanging out, socks at all levels, hands and knees dirty and satchel dragging on the ground. Yet he was the serious one, worrying about problems which often existed only in his mind. He read whenever he could, hiding away in some corner of the barn. His sense of humour was much more subtle than that of John.

Basil and Mary followed more quietly. Basil was the odd one out of the three brothers, more timid and not so adventurous, but truthful and honest, qualities not appreciated by the other two as part of his honesty was to tell Mum everything the older brothers did wrong. It earned him many a sore head. He was devoted to Mum and found his great pleasure in doing chores for her, much to the disgust of John and Constantin, who dodged all that they could.

Mary, the oldest sister, took it upon herself to be in charge of Sanda and me. She was often domineering with it. "That's not the right way to do it, I'll show you how" or "*Mama* says you're to feed the hens". I resented her giving me orders and acting as though she knew it all, but I had to suffer it for Mum would always back her up.

But despite their quirks I loved my brothers and sisters dearly. Each one had a special warm place in my heart. When we came later to be separated there was an eternal emptiness within me that nothing seemed to fill.

Ephraim, my half brother, was eighteen and refused to look upon John or Constantin as equals. He had a chip on his shoulder about them, thinking that he was hard done by to have to work on the farm, while the other two were either playing or dodging the farm jobs. He thought them lazy and mostly ignored them, which annoyed the two brothers when they were older and at college. It also annoyed Mum.

"Why do you treat them like that, Ephraim?" "Because they think themselves superior to me! John struts about like a peacock preening his feathers, and Constantin thinks he knows it all. Why can't one of them stay home and work on the farm as I do?" "Oh, Ephraim, I think you are being silly. You know you had your chance of college, but didn't bother to study hard enough. John and Constantin have worked well to pass their exams, and deserve to better themselves. I'll do what I can for them and for the others when they are old enough".

I came to understand Ephraim later, for although Mum sent the boys to do various chores, such as looking after the cows and horses, moving the ducks and geese to fresh grass, gathering sunflower stalks and twigs for cooking fuel or taking food to the men working in the fields, they could never resist the temptation of slipping away to play, whenever there was the chance, especially to the wonderful playground of the river and the hanging ropes of willows along its banks.

We girls would join them. It was idyllic in the warm sun, with tucked up skirt and bare feet, to wade about in the shallows with the cool water swirling and bubbling beneath my toes. Mary, Sanda and I played only in the safer parts, leaving all the daring to the boys who ventured into the deeper river, trousers rolled up, to try, always unsuccessfully, to catch the darting fish, much too quick to be caught by clumsy hands.

Placed across the river was a single plank bridge, put there for the convenience of the adults, but the boys used it for any purpose except the correct one. They hung to it with their hands and waded through the depths, using the plank as support. It could be a boundary to their territories, or some sort of cave beneath which to hide, or some other figment of their imagination. Naturally we were often wet, but the hot sun soon dried us out.

Sanda, once becoming a little too bold, followed Basil and Constantin across the plank. When she was halfway across both jumped up and down on the bridge to make fun of her. They succeeded so well that she fell off into the water and became soaked.

Scared and wet she was pulled out by Constantin who desperately tried to calm her and quieten her screams, apprehensive that Mum would hear and come to stop the fun.

The willows along the bank were the boy's jungle, where they searched for bird's nests, and climbed high to jump down into the water, creating splashes which they hoped would engulf us all, but usually managing no more than to get themselves saturated. It was also a vantage point, up high, to give directions as to the whereabouts of the fish.

"Over there, Basil, under that rock. It's huge!" shouted Constantin. "A bit further along, no, just there. Oh, you clumsy idiot, you've lost it now!"

Most of the time we girls were left to play in the farmyard. Mary and I spent hours making dolls from corn cobs and dressing them in scraps of material, or threading maize seeds or beans into necklaces, or just imitating the ways of the adults. With pieces of stick and string we spun and wove or prepared flax. Cleaning and cooking, and looking after babies were our mainstays. Most of all I liked to borrow some of Mum's old clothes and shoes, dress up, and force myself to stagger around in footwear several sizes too large. When we were old enough to attend, weddings and funerals represented great occasions for us, for not only were the real ceremonies exciting, but the three of us were provided with food for our imaginations for ages afterwards. We could be brides, bridesmaids, priests, or whatever we chose.

One great delight, when the crop ripened, was provided by the huge mulberry tree which grew by the orchard fence. All of us, except John, who hated getting his hands stained, joined in the great tasty game of fun and feasting. Constantin and Basil climbed into the tree and picked the fruit, pushing it directly into their sticky, juice stained mouths, while Mary, Sanda and I, being much smaller, stayed on the ground and scrabbled for the fruit which had fallen, or had been shaken down with the action of the boys in the branches. We had to eat quickly, for the ducks and geese milling around also liked mulberries and made it quite plain that they were more entitled to the fruit than any frilly human offspring.

The mulberries, similar in shape to loganberries, were black and beautifully sweet. They had to be eaten immediately for they deteriorated rapidly in the summer heat. When the crop was ripe the berries fell in multitudes, covering the ground in a purple carpet. The fruit underneath squashed and fermented, and in the darkness and warmth must have produced some form of alcohol, for one day we were astonished to see the ducks and geese, who had been eating their fill from early morning, staggering about on uncertain legs of rubber.

Some fell over and slowly wobbled up again, necks limp and bent, eyes unfocussed and half closed. Their wings flapped clumsily and uncoordinatedly. Many eventually toppled on their sides and lay as though dead, not being able to resist our catching them. Even the ones still standing could only aim vague inaccurate pecks at us. They were as drunk as any of the old men of the village ever became. I now wonder whether they suffered hangovers the next day.

The first time I ever left the yard to go into the village was when Mum decided to take me to her sister Alexandra, who lived at the far end of the community. I trotted behind, head turning in all directions, looking with curiosity at the small farms and houses which were dotted about in no orderly fashion, with tracks winding, like a maze, between them. Most of the houses were painted white and had roofs of coarse thatch, almost all topped by a huge stork's nest, as was ours also.

When we reached the house of Auntie Alexandra, Mum opened the gate and marched me in, giving no heed to the resident dog, which had naturally started to bark, racing up and down its length of wire. Hearing the noise brought my aunt into the garden to greet us, calling "*tsiba*, *tsiba*" to the dog to cease its useless barking. After the two sisters embraced, my aunt said, "Come into the house where it is much cooler". We entered a large room, where Mum sat down thankfully, wiping perspiration from her face. She pulled me gently to sit on her lap.

My aunt went into the next room, while still keeping the conversation with Mum flowing, and returned with a tray bearing three small dishes holding a conserve made from whole bitter cherries in a thick syrup. Naturally, I was the first to finish this treat, traditionally offered to guests, together with a glass of water, in the hot summer months.

"Lia, go now to the field behind the farm and play with Theodora who is watching the chicks for me", said my aunt.

Glad to be released from the dull adult conversation I hopped noisily down the steps, which started the dog barking again. Frightened I retreated quickly to the house, forcing Auntie to come out and lead me by the hand past the growling hound. "Here, follow this path to the end of the garden, then climb over the stile".

As I mounted the wooden structure I looked over the top, and my breath was taken away by the huge panorama which stretched before me. I just could not believe it. Sloping away into the distance were fields and orchards, meadows and vineyards, a massive jigsaw of multiple greens. In the hazy farawayness the houses of another village showed mistily. What had suddenly happened to the only small world I knew so far? Here I was faced with a place where the sky had moved away in front of me, meeting fields well beyond the other village. I was confused and bewildered for all the perspectives had changed in an instant. Standing on the stile, motionless, I was astonished and a little stunned by the vastness of it all. My wonderment was interrupted by hearing my name called.

"Lia, Lia, come here, I'm so glad to see you, I'm bored staying with these silly chicks". I descended and ran towards my cousin, scattering chicks on the way. I knew Theodora, having seen her before at our house. She was, as I, barefoot, with a light grey dress made in the same simple style as were those made by Mum for Mary, Sanda and me: square neck, short sleeves and skirt gathered at the sides of the waist.

We lay for a while on the grass, chattering and watching the chicks, both joining in the task of keeping them out of the cultivated area. It was an unending battle of wills between the little creatures and us. They had the fixed idea of getting into the vegetable plot; Theodora and I, armed with willow twigs, had to keep them out.

As a diversion, my cousin showed me a game of hers which was to lie out straight, arms at the sides, and roll down the hill. After two or three failures I succeeded rolling faster each time, until I ended in a bed of nettles, which sent me back to Mum, with arms full of stings.

Once back home Mary asked me curiously, "How was it at Auntie Alexandra's?" Full of excitement I immediately launched into my story, trying to describe all the new things I had seen on the way. How astonished I had been by the panorama at the back of the garden, with the fields stretching for such a distance. How there the sky was so vast, not reaching the land until it passed the next village, not, as on our farm, ending at the field opposite.

"I saw so many houses before we reached Auntie's", I said

proudly, as though only I could have seen such a number. With her seniority of years and her superior knowledge Mary replied scornfully, "You are silly! of course there are a lot of other houses and farms, you have no idea how the village looks, but I know all about it. I know how to get to *Bunica* (Grannie) and even to Cigoreni (the village I saw in the panorama), and as for Auntie Alexandra, I bet I could get there even in the dark!"

Losing my own cosy little world upset me a lot, but nowhere near as much as becoming an aunt at my young age. This had happened the first time when I was two years old, and the stork had brought George and Marika a baby girl named Anouska, but at that time I was unaware of my new status. Later, after another three years, they had a boy and this time I was very conscious of it.

"You are an aunt again, Lia, what do you think about that?" asked Mum, happily. What I thought made me burst into tears. All my aunts were grown up and elderly and I did not want to be classed with them.

"Why are you crying, my love?" asked Mum at my unexpected reaction. When I told her how I felt she tried to cheer me up.

"I know it's most unusual to be an aunt at your age, but it's a lot of fun and you should be happy about it!" I was reassured to some extent by Mum's words, and decided to accept the situation.

"Come and see your nephew", Marika invited me cheerfully when Mum took me on a visit shortly after the birth. I went close to the bed shyly, with a touch of apprehension to see such a small creature, with closed eyes and face as red as a lobster, wrapped in a blanket. On his forehead he had a band with a tiny cross sewn into it.

"Wah, wah", the little fellow who had made me an aunt responded to my gentle touch. Seeing he was wet Marika began to change him. I watched with curiosity as under the blanket, which had been fastened envelope fashion and tied with a ribbon, was revealed a wee figure wrapped in bands of material, wound all the way from shoulders to feet. No arms or legs could be seen, just the closed eyes in the red face and the little bound Egyptian mummy figure below. Marika unwrapped the swaddling bands and eventually beneath all this was the baby boy. She replaced the soiled nappy with a fresh one and repacked him with all the bands, the enveloping blanket and finally the ribbon.

"Why do you tie him up like that?" I asked, inquisitively. In her warm slow musical voice Marika answered. "Because I want him to grow straight, and not have bandy legs like Pavel Dimitriu", naming a character in the village who had deformed limbs. She continued. "You yourself were swaddled like this when you were small, and you have straight legs, haven't you?" Later I saw many other babies being bound in the same fashion until they were about five months old, after which the bands were used just to keep the nappies in position, the arms being allowed free. I learned that the little cross on the forehead was supposed to keep away evil spirits.

I remember the happiness exuding from Marika's face as she looked down at the little boy, with her large brown eyes so full of love. She was now about twenty three, with very dark hair which accentuated her pale skin. She wore her hair tightly combed back, exposing her wide forehead. Marika was one of my favourite persons, often visiting us and telling me stories with patience and love. She seemed very intelligent and liked to read a great deal, sometimes to the detriment of her housework. Some of her friends were teachers, with whom she could converse easily on serious subjects, despite her having had less education than they. The marriage she had with George was a good one. He was accepted by her parents as a true son. To them my half brother was a great asset with his penchant for hard work and his love of agriculture. I saw him less than Marika, but he was always kind and seemed so wise. He was as tall as Dad, resembling him in his looks, with his high cheekbones and slavic features. His warm broad smile charmed everyone. We youngsters loved him, for he always had so much time for us. Unlike Dad he had no moustache, which he thought old fashioned, and unlike Ephraim he was never at odds with Mum. In fact I never heard him utter a bad word about anyone.

When we went to the christening of Boris, the baby, I heard Mum whisper to Auntie Mary "Marika and George were christened on the same day, in the very same water. Wasn't it a strange co-incidence that they should marry each other, and at only eighteen?"

During the service Boris was taken out of his nappy and immersed completely in the holy water, the priest covering the little fellows nose and mouth with his hand to prevent him breathing in any of the liquid. Afterwards at the house a feast had been prepared, and later Marika examined happily all the presents which had been given to the baby: many swaddling bands, mostly embroidered, napkins, little blankets, a frontal band with a sewn-in cross and many other useful items.

"I am going to give my first grandson a foal, so that when he is capable of riding he will have his own horse!" announced Dad grandly. I heard afterwards that Mum had given Anouska a carpet for her christening, a well appreciated first contribution to her 'bottom drawer'. I later enjoyed going to many christenings, as my parents were often asked by village couples to be godparents as a mark of respect. Sometimes to the poorer ones Dad gave a calf or a piglet.

When I was about five my paternal grandfather died. I remember little about him except that he was an imposing man with a long white beard. Now he was in an open coffin laid on the bed of the guest room. Flowers were arranged about his head, arms folded across his chest and a small ikon placed on his hands. It looked to me as though he was just sleeping. He was kept in the room for three days, as tradition demanded, with a lit candle by his head, while relatives and friends kept a constant vigil.

On the day of the funeral the coffin, still open, was carried into the yard, now crammed full of mourners. The procession moved off slowly to the church and, after the service, to the cemetery. During the journey twenty four stops were made, symbolising the 'steps to heaven', with many gifts being distributed at each stop 'for the soul of my grandfather'. All about me relatives were weeping and lamenting, making me feel sad without realising the loss. The priest made the sign of the cross over the body of my *Bunicu*, then the coffin was closed and nailed and lowered into the ground. Clods of earth drummed a last farewell on the lid.

After the funeral Dad learned that *Bunicu's* farm and property had all been left to him. There was naturally a lot of discussion in the family following this bequest, one of the problems being that Grannie was still living at the farm. She was quite an old infirm lady, needing a stick to help her move about, so it was resolved, with her agreement, that she would go to stay with her daughter Liuba, who lived not far away.

My father made several visits to the farm, and as it was very much better in many ways than ours, he decided we should move there. On that farm, as well as the main large house, there was an old cottage, quite dilapidated, which Dad intended to demolish and replace with a new barn and summer kitchen.

On his next visit I went with him and, to my surprise and obviously to that of Dad, on a rickety chair in front of the old house was sitting my grannie, a little shrivelled figure with a lined face and grey hair, dressed from head to foot in black, clutching her walking stick. She was supposed to be living now with her daughter.

"Hello, Mum", said my father in a surprised voice, "I didn't expect to see you here!".

"Why not?" replied Grannie, "I live here".

"I thought it was settled that you are going to live with Liuba?" queried Dad.

"Yes, it was, but I've changed my mind, I've decided to stay here in the old house".

It all seemed a bit silly to me for the house was little more than a ruin. I left Dad trying to pacify his mother while I wandered off on a trip of discovery. Shortly after I could hear Grannie's voice raised in shrill anger and looking back I saw the reason. Two men, bringing a ladder, propped it against the house, climbed up and began to strip the thatch from the roof, obviously on my father's instructions. At this outrage Grannie was protesting loudly, shaking her stick and screaming furiously at Dad. "May you rot in prison for this!" She threatened the men with her dangerous stick and told them to get off the roof of her house, an order which they ignored.

Later, when Dad had been deported, I came to remember Grannie's curse and hated her for it.

Once we were home Dad related the day's events to Mum, who was very upset by the way Grannie had acted.

I cannot remember how long it was before we moved to the new farm, but it must have been a few weeks, for when we arrived both the new barn and the summer kitchen were built, with roofs of white tiles, and the old house had disappeared as though it had never been.

"Where's *Bunica*?" I wanted to know, remembering the argument.

"She has gone to live with Auntie Liuba", replied Dad. I was pleased that all must have worked out well, not knowing then of the politics which exist in all families.

At this time my parents were still young, just in their early forties and very happy with their lot. Mum was of medium height, not by any means slim, for having had six children had padded her figure out somewhat, but neither was she fat, just cuddly. Her beautiful smooth skin, darkened a little by the sun, set off her expressive green eyes, which reflected her character, full of joy and always cheerful. Her delicate oval face was topped by light brown hair, which she combed back into a bun. In the week the practicalities of living on a farm dictated her dress, usually a long pleated skirt, dark coloured, a flowered white blouse with sleeveless corselletted top, finished off with an apron. Footwear varied from open sandals in the summer to fur lined boots in the winter.

Dad was different in character and outlook. He was serious minded and planned as far ahead as he could. Tall, slim and wiry, with corded muscles on his tanned body, he worked hard in his beloved fields with the idea of buying enough land to give each of us about ten hectares, when we married. If he had any spare time he preferred to sit at home quietly, whereas Mum loved giving parties and taking any opportunity to go to the *Hora*, the village folk dances. I adored my father and a hug from him was a precious thing to look forward to. I took it for granted that Mum would cuddle and comfort me any time. Our parents were overjoyed at what they had so far achieved. We all loved our new home in which we lived happily until tragedy overtook us. The stables and the coach house, the new and old barns and the summer kitchen made quite an impressive property, built for a wealthy family. The house was grand compared with those on the old farm. It had a small front garden protected by a low pretty fence which kept out the chickens and geese. Here, every spring, Mum was bent double setting out the bedding plants. She loved to grow sweet basil which she dried and hung in bunches in the cupboards and near the ikons to give a pleasant scent through the house. The six rooms were large, with white lace curtains at every window, beautiful hand made carpets on all the walls, and ikons, some plated with gold, hung in each corner. Under these, every Sunday and Saint's day, Mum lit the small votive lamps, or sometimes a candle. We children were told to kneel and pray in our rooms in front of the ikons.

One room was very large and used solely for parties and guests. Here a massive table with curved legs surrounded by heavy carved chairs occupied the whole space by the two large windows. A chest of drawers stood in one corner surmounted by a very ornamented samovar of fine copper.

I shared a bedroom with Mary and Sanda, while the boys had their own room. In winter I liked to sleep occasionally on top of the huge tiled stove, specially constructed with flat areas where mattresses could be placed. It was so warm and cosy high up, facing a window to the garden, where the outside temperature was often minus thirty degrees Celsius.

On this farm the cellar was a separate construction beside the house. It had been made by digging out a large space and roofing it over before covering it with the dug earth. One end was built up higher than the other to allow for a door and from its appearance I thought of it as a monster with a big mouth.

Once our family had settled in, Mum called the priest to bless the house, as tradition required. It was another Sunday best day, as with such an event many relatives and friends came to the ceremony. The priest and his verger entered the first room where they began holding a service, the holy man swinging his censer with the smoking incense all about him, then walking through the house, dipping a bunch of sweet basil into the holy water and flicking it into every corner, calling down blessings as he went. When the ceremony ended, the adults sat down to a long table piled high with delicacies to eat, drink and be merry, while we children, with all our various cousins, were sent into the summer kitchen and left to eat under John's supervision.

TWO

In the new house, securely blessed against all evils, we started a new phase in our lives. Soon after moving, between the old and new barns, Dad fixed a wire for a dog which someone had given to us. It quickly adopted the habit of all the other village dogs of running madly on its length of chain up and down the wire, barking at all comers. I have no idea what breed it was, but it grew to about the size of a labrador. It was white with many brown spots. John, to be different, called it Bob. It was unusual to name dogs, who were not considered pets in any way but just regarded as guard animals.

On this farm my parents seemed to be more enthusiastic than ever, Dad working in the fields for all the hours God sent, and Mum helping him as much as she could apart from the household tasks. Every day except Sunday, for that was a day of rest and the day I loved.

The morning started with the bell in the church tower calling everyone to the service. This was the day when Mum took the opportunity to wear something more in fashion, her favourite dress being of a dark cherry red velvet, decorated with little silver squares, together with her high heeled patent leather shoes. I can visualise her on her way to church, her head proudly erect, her eyes bright and challenging, a sure sign she was pleased with her family of seven, all dressed in their best clothes, each of us girls similarly outfitted to show the world that we belonged to her.

Dad, tall, slim and handsome, with his curly black hair, thick eyebrows and trimmed moustache looked so elegant in his dark suit, white shirt and pale blue tie, more like one of the intellectuals than a peasant farmer. Mum always checked his dress, wanting him to be 'presentable'! She had a great sense of family position in the village and was quite determined that none of us, including Dad, would let her down. Despite her carefree manner she had an ambitious streak for her family. Both of my parents were well respected in the community, regarded as a kind and generous couple who could be relied on for sympathy and help.

They were very religious, their lives being ruled by their strong beliefs and their complete faith in the Lord. Mum did her best to bring us up with a subtle mixture of religion, tradition and plain commonsense. Faith, hope and charity about summed up their philosophy, for faith they had in plenty, hope for all of us and charity in that no one who came knocking at the door for help was turned away empty handed. They believed absolutely that their lives were ordained and guided by God. But their faith was to be sorely tried before very long.

As we walked to the church, it made me proud to see so many men doffing their hats to Dad as we passed. We entered quietly the blue, gold and red of the holy interior, lit only by the flickering groups of candles standing in the trays of sand, passing a few ikons of the saints on our way to our allotted places.

Men and women stood separately, Dad facing the altar, reflecting his status as the most respected man in the village. The boys stayed with him. Mum placed herself opposite her favourite ikon of St. Nicholas, and we girls sat with her.

At my young age I did not like the service, for it seemed interminable. Moreover, I could not follow the words of the priest, and to add to my discomfort I had to kneel from time to time on rough hessian mats which tortured me by digging sharp fibres into my flesh. To relieve the pain I sometimes relaxed from the stiff upright position and sank back onto my haunches. Unfortunately Mum had sharp eyes for any such deviation and after a few minutes of relative comfort I received a silent but painful dig in my side from a rigid finger, with a whispered, "Sit properly upright, will you!" which returned me to my straight back and painful knees posture.

I paid little attention to anything that was said in the service, my time being filled with looking at the ikons, the scenes of bible stories painted on the interior of the church and at the other children in the congregation who were just about as inattentive and bored as I was.

When, at long last, the service was over, the verger came with his dish into which everyone dropped money. I was given small coins to place in the tray and this was my favourite time, placing my coins importantly on the plate and trying to estimate how many were there already.

Once out in the churchyard the adults stayed with relatives and friends for a general discussion. Mum and Dad found someone to chat with, and now all the tension of kneeling or standing straight had gone I ran eagerly to join other children playing around the church. Family groups split away and slowly meandered towards their houses for lunch. I regarded Sunday lunchtime as a heavenly period!

The long carved table was set with an impeccable white lace cloth, all china and cutlery laid out ready. As we entered the house, neat and clean from the Saturday scrubbing, flowers arranged about the room greeted us. The glorious smell of Mum's cooking started me drooling and we children scrambled for our places at the table. We sat in our best clothes, with large knapkins spread on our laps to protect them, while Mum and Mary served the delicious meal.

When the lunch ended and all had been cleared, Dad relaxed in his favourite chair on the verandah. I took the opportunity of climbing up on his knee, for him to put an arm affectionately about me and cuddle me. Once, when I reached up and touched his thick dark hair, he murmured, as if to himself. "My little Lia, I wonder what we'll make of you in this troubled world?". I just loved the feel of his strong arm holding me, his warm body, the faint lavender or basil smell of his clothes. I did not understand his rhetorical question, but I was used to adults saying incomprehensible things. Certainly at my age there was no trouble in my world. I was sitting on my adored father's knee, his protective arm about me. Mum, my fountain of comfort and love, was somewhere in the house. My three brothers were growing up straight and strong. Ephraim seemed kind to me. I had Mary to teach me all she knew and I had Sanda, whom I helped Mum look after. No, my world was not troubled. How could I even imagine at that time what was to befall me and my family.

Ephraim was happy on Sundays as he had the chance to go out, especially when he was courting a girl from the village. The other three brothers noisily played in the yard at some game or other, while Mary helped in the kitchen. Sometimes Mum came on to the verandah, holding Sanda in her arms and interrupted my daydreams.

"Lia, love, go out and play, leave your dad alone, he wants to rest". I reluctantly slipped from his lap.

"Yes", he said, "I'll have a few minutes. Nicola will you tell the boys to take the horses to the field, give them some exercise, they like doing that".

"I'll tell them, I'm going to sit out front with Mary" replied Mum.

The brothers, clothes changed, went off with the two horses, taking me with them. Untaught, all the other boys and my brothers picked up riding from copying the adults. I liked to sit on the grass and watch quietly as the horses trotted up and down the meadow with make believe cossacks on their backs, until the animals had had enough and started to graze. The boys then tied them to the nearest tree with lengths of rope, to prevent them straying, and went back to the ever attractive river.

So Sunday passed, with only the minimum of essential work being done, but in weekdays, especially in the spring, there was always such feverish activity.

"Basil", ordered Mum. "Go and get the chicken baskets". Basil dutifully dragged out a dozen of the large wicker baskets from the barn.

"Now you two". That was Mary and I. "Fill them with straw". I knew what to do but Mary liked to supervise.

"There's too much in that one, not enough in that. That one's quite empty. . ." She had to be the boss, just because she was older.

When satisfied Mum put eggs in each one, after holding them in front of a lamp to see that they were fertile.

"Now take the full baskets to the barn. You, Basil and Mary had better carry them, they're too heavy for Lia". There were always too many baskets to find places for them all in the barn and eventually a few overflowed into the summer kitchen.

"Put them under the seats, the carpets will hide them out of the way". That was the plank seats, covered with rugs, that could serve for beds if necessary. As the hens became broody they were set on the baskets where they stayed content until the eggs were hatched. We had great interest in this for each basket was supposedly under our individual care. "These are yours, Lia. These for you, Mary", and so on. I eagerly awaited the hatching time to see which one of us had done the best. If all my eggs hatched I was very proud, having done exactly nothing to help the miracle.

The hens under the seats produced lots of laughs. When anyone came to visit, one of the boys, John or Constantin, would say.

"Sit over there, Auntie Mary, it's out of the draught", or some such reason or other. The visitor sat, thinking, or even saying to Mum.

"Your boys are very polite, so well mannered". That was until the hen under the seat got bored and pecked at the nearest object, which just happened to be Auntie's leg. There was a scream of alarm, and the unfortunate visitor jumped up, rubbing her leg, with us all, who had been waiting in anticipation, roaring with laughter. Quite often, for the birds were so quiet, I was myself caught, through forgetfully sitting on the seat.

I was given and proudly accepted the job of feeding the growing chicks, which meant collecting beetroot leaves and nettles, cutting them into small pieces and mixing them with crushed maize. One of my pleasures was to watch the new young animals appear from all corners of the farm at this time of creation. A young foal on thin spindly legs, brown and white mooing calves, litters of pink piglets, goslings and ducklings galore clustered in little families.

My brothers helped at the busy time, but not too eagerly, with the exception of Basil, who was always working. I often heard Dad asking.

"Where's John? I need him to help Ephraim with the cart this afternoon".

"I don't know where he is Dad, I haven't seen him", replied Constantin innocently. I thought him very naughty for I knew he was fibbing and Mum always taught us it was wicked and a sin not to tell the truth.

Basil, who had been carrying water for Mum, heard the question. "He's in the barn, Dad".

"What's he doing there?"

"He's lifting weights". Constantin shot a black look at his talkative brother.

"What do you mean, lifting weights?"

"He lifts the weights from the scales, you know, to give him big muscles, thinks he's going to be an Atlas one day", said Ephraim sarcastically.

"There are plenty of things to lift about on this farm without weights, but I don't see him doing that. You'd better get him to help you with those sacks, Ephraim, use his muscles to some advantage". Dad called Constantin just as he was about so slide out of sight. "You too, young man. Go with Ephraim, there's something you can do to help him, I'm sure". Basil had retreated into the kitchen, avoiding any further threatening looks from Constantin.

Together with the fresh green leaves and the bursting buds came Easter. I always loved so much the procession in which all the villagers took part, everyone holding a lighted candle, an atmosphere of just pure magic.

After the service came the food blessing ceremony, another great enjoyment for me. The congregation formed a double line all round the church, the lines facing inwards. Each family had in front of them a wicker basket lined with beautifully embroidered cloths, containing eggs, hard boiled and coloured for the occasion, a bottle of wine and a special Easter cake.

Filled with excitement I watched intently as the priest and a verger, followed by the singing choir, walked between the two lines, the people parting in front of them like two waves. The verger carried a bowl of holy water and the priest a bunch of sweet basil, which he dipped in the water and flicked at each basket as he passed, murmuring all the while his Easter blessing.

After the ritual we went home to start our meal with the food which had been blessed. At this time in the dining room there was always a bowl of eggs which Mum had coloured. Some red, some blue, some green and many with the most intricate patterns, showing Mum's artistic flair and great patience. The most attractively decorated eggs were usually kept for the guests.

Easter lunch always began for some reason with eggs coloured red, then lamb soup, followed by a dish of lamb stuffed with herbs. More dishes with a lamb base came next, finished off with an Easter cheese-cake.

As children we had great fun from cracking the eggs as tradition required. In pairs we selected eggs from the dish, both holding one in a fist, with just the end of the egg showing. Then the opponent banged his or her egg down on that of the challenger, saying, "Jesus has risen from his tomb", to which the reply was "It is true Jesus has risen". Whoever cracked the other egg then claimed it for himself. That day my brothers usually came home with pockets full of cracked eggs.

Amongst the boys were all sorts of recipes for hardening the shells and the method John and Constantin favoured was to bury the eggs in manure for a few days. This, they swore, hardened the shell considerably. Whether it did or not their score of eggs was always high.

No Easter passed without Mum making or buying new clothes for us all. Although reach-me-downs were good enough for play, Easter was the time for new dresses for the girls and suits for the boys, as well as new shoes. I so loved this time, to be dressed in pretty new clothes.

During one of these holy days a wandering musician with an accordion or fiddle was bound to call at the village. When he started to play the tunes for a *Hora*, the folk dances began in the village square. The dancing continued for as long as the man was able to play, with most of the youngsters and many not so young joining in and showing their prowess. The music excited me and I wished at the time to be older and dance like them.

Sometimes a photographer with a big box camera, a tripod and a case of equipment appeared. He was at once in great demand as all the families wanted photographs taken, and ours was no exception. Once Mum had managed to catch him, she brought him to the house, sat him comfortably with a jug of wine and some *cozonac* (a sort of pound cake), while she sorted us out.

She laid a carpet in front of the house and all the family, including grannies, grandads, aunts, uncles and cousins were positioned on it.

"You, Lia, Mary and Sanda, in front with your cousins, then all the boys behind. Dad, you go there at the back, Auntie Mary next to Dad. . ." and so on until she was satisfied, then proudly took her place beside Dad, leaving the expert to proceed.

I thought the photographer must be some sort of magician as he fiddled about under his black cloth, then re-appeared with a little rubber bulb in his hand.

"All stay still!" As the others I held my breath, worried lest I should move, and remained like a statue for a few seconds until the bulb was pressed and I could relax and breathe again. Weeks later the photographer returned with his finished prints, another joyful day when everyone joined in with praise or criticism. Another large jug of wine for the expert. If every family did the same I wonder that anything was in focus, but finally we had another framed picture of the family, once again all looking as serious as wooden statues.

Life carried on quietly and orderly after we had settled in the new farm. Whilst in Europe the sabre rattling of Hitler had increased, in our village nothing seemed to change and no one knew how soon it would. There was little outside influence. The one telephone was in the house of the mayor, who lived in the next larger village. Newspapers were only regularly obtained by the priest and the teachers. Letters were sent via the mayor's house by anyone who was passing. There were very few radio receivers and not much news was broadcast, anyway.

There was no public transport, no electricity, no running water, refuse collections or sewerage, and other than the news which occasionally filtered down from the priest or one of the teachers very little reached us about the outside world.

Most of the local news was brought by the crier, the greater part being local edicts. This man came to the village either on Sunday or in the evenings when the villagers were back from the fields. Around his waist a belt supported a small drum, on which he beat out a certain rhythm with little sticks. As a girl I was very amused by the crier. As soon as I heard the drum I rushed to see this funny man striding down the road, followed by a horde of laughing children. 'Tarrum, tarrum', sounded the drum, then a pause while the man shouted his message. The children all stopped with him.

"The vineyard taxes must be paid by this Friday! School will restart on Monday at eight o'clock! The public notary will attend in the mayor's house from nine until one o'clock next Thursday, etc, etc." Then he strode off, followed by the army of tots all imitating his walk and beating silent drums, until a hundred yards along he halted again and repeated his performance.

Nearby our new farm was the only shop in the village, run by a Jewish family. The little general store sold most of the necessities of life which could not be made or grown on the farm. The family owning the shop consisted of three persons: Isaac, the husband, his wife Rachael and their daughter Anka, an unusual name in our village. They spoke with an accent different from that of the local people, and this was naturally fastened on by the children, who thought it very funny. Mum shopped there for items she urgently needed but in general all that we wanted from outside the farm was bought by my parents when they went into the town of Orhei on one of their rare shopping trips. These were always made with the chief objective of buying bulk stores, as cakes of salt for the animals, paraffin for the lamps, tools or items of farm equipment, or combined with the journeys Dad made when he had grain to sell in the market. Mum took the opportunity to look for such things as shoes, buttons, threads, elastic, crockery, glassware and other household goods.

I waited impatiently, with great emotion and anticipation, for them to return from these expeditions. If my father went alone he always brought back something unusual or different, such as *Halva* (a sort of sweetmeat made from almonds), pretzels or small sticks of white bread, which he said was bread from the rabbits, leaving me puzzled. Sweets, too, were a very special treat for us. When Mum went with him I knew we might get shoes, or perhaps a shop-bought dress which had caught her fancy. Then on Sunday I and my sisters would be able to parade them through the village on the way to church.

At regular intervals Dad loaded his cart with sacks of maize or wheat to have them ground into flour in the next village. This milling was almost always a days work, because the mill, driven by a horse walking a roundabout, worked neither fast nor very efficiently. The owner provided only the machine and the horsepower. Dad had to feed the corn into the hopper and bag the resultant flour. He often returned late, covered from head to foot in white dust. His floured curly hair and face looked like that of a circus clown, causing us to burst into fits of laughter.

Mum, knowing that the mill, as it happens, was run by a woman, would say, jokingly.

"Late again, that miller's wife must have some attractions I haven't got to keep you there so long!"

Great happy events for us were the occasional trips as a family for pure enjoyment, to visit relatives, to take part in a wedding or a christening or going to a market. There had to be a very good reason indeed to prevent Mum going to a wedding or a christening. They were the spice of life to her.

Then came the day when I had to leave Mum's side and go to school. That was in September 1939, when the war in Europe had begun. Of course I was then much too young to understand what was happening.

In Romania, not yet directly involved in the conflict, King Carol was still on the throne. Hungary was demanding the region of Transylvania and Russia wanted Bessarabia, causing Carol to turn to Hitler for help. As a result an agreement signed in March 1939 gave Germany 'exceptional privileges'. In the same month Hitler invaded Czechoslovakia. Later that year Stalin and Hitler signed a non-agression pact, and on August twenty third Hitler agreed that Stalin could have Bessarabia. This last agreement was signed in secrecy, neither Carol nor the Romanian people knowing of its existence. On September the first, Germany invaded Poland and triggered off the war.

If anyone had mentioned a war it meant nothing to me. I had the excitement of going to school for the first time. Already I knew a lot about it from my brothers and sister Mary, but knowing was one thing and experiencing it another.

When the term began Mum dressed me in a pretty pinafore dress, with a ribbon in my hair, and led me to the gate, where Dad waited to take me to the school. With some apprehension and a little touch of fear churning in my stomach I carried my new slate in my new shoulder bag, walking proudly along the tracks, with my adored father holding my hand.

Once we reached the school Dad kissed me on the forehead and left me with the waiting teacher. Anna, my girl neighbour, was also there and I happily greeted her. The teacher, seeing that I had found a friend, left me in order to go about her other duties.

At eight o'clock the bell rang summoning us all to the entrance, to be led into the classroom two by two. Anna and I sat together at a double desk awaiting the teacher opening the register and calling our names. When I heard mine I jumped up and repeated 'present' as I had seen the others do, very pleased with myself for having cleared the first hurdle without mistake.

Our basic education started with making shapes and marks on the squeaky slates, to help us later with writing letters and numbers. These we learned one at a time until we triumphantly mastered the alphabet.

Once the whole class had attained this ability, notebooks were allowed, in which writing with pencil was first permitted, graduating to pens dipped in little pots of ink set into the desk. The ink had the habit of creeping up my fingers, which did not please Mum one little bit, for she had to get the stains out of my clothes each washday.

Reading, writing and arithmetic were the principal subjects, with later some needlework for the girls. The teacher, a tall auburn haired lady with glasses and a stern look, always carried a wicked looking cane, which she ceremoniously laid on the desk before her. If anyone was outrageously naughty he or she would be given a smart stroke across each palm, but it very rarely occurred. Standing in a corner with hands on head was a more common punishment.

At home Mary and Basil strictly checked my efforts, considering themselves already expert in the three R's. By now Constantin and John had said goodbye to the primary school and had been sent to study in the college in Orhei. They came home at holiday times, noses lifted in the air with their superiority, for very few of the village children had the good fortune to be sent to any form of higher education. But my parents were determined that their children would not follow the traditional role of back breaking farm work. Mum had a dream that the boys would become teachers and the girls marry priests. Being brought up in a remote peasant village these two professions represented the highest echelons of society that Mum knew, and for us all to fulfil her dream would be the pinnacle of success. She made no secret of her plans, telling her ambitions to relatives and friends. If she did this in my hearing I would cringe with embarrassment, hiding behind her skirts at each mention of marriage, although I had no conception of its full meaning.

"When you grow up, Lia, Mum will marry you to a priest and you will have no need to work in the fields", she would say, combing my hair or trying a new dress on my small figure. The priests of her dreams evidently had no choice in the matter.

The attainment of these ambitions was the spur that stimulated Mum and Dad into working from dawn until dusk, to buy more land for our dowries or obtain more money to keep John and Constantin, and later Basil and Mary in college. It was a cruel irony that this very ambition of becoming more prosperous was to end later in the loss of all they had worked for.

John was now about seventeen and tall for his age, slim, but just beginning to develop his adult frame. Ever joyful, he kept himself and everyone else in fits of laughter by his funny jokes. He continued to be keen on sport, pre-occupied with his figure and proud of his long tapering hands. He was, as usual, neat and tidy in his appearance, his clothes pressed and spotless. Constantin had by now developed a keen sense of observation. He spent hours reading and studying. At this age he was clever artistically, making animal figures in clay or wood, drawing and painting. I even remember him working for ages to make an enlargement of a photo of Mum, with some basic equipment he had managed to borrow. Proud of her son's talent Mum happily showed the picture to everyone. Later in life photography became his passion. Clothes were not so important to him as to John. The closeness which existed between them did not extend to any other member of the family. To listen to their arguments would mislead anyone who did not know of the bond uniting them, which was to stay with them for the rest of their lives.

When they were home on holiday I listened with fascination to the stories they told us about the college and life in the town, things I had never seen or imagined. They also pleased us girls with bringing little presents, mostly sweets, sometimes socks or a beret, but once John brought me a pair of gloves, so pretty and different from anything in the village.

The two brothers were prepared to enjoy a holiday of rest and play, but after they had spent a few days doing practically nothing except kick a ball about the yard Dad thought it time they did some work on the farm.

"John, go and give Ephraim a hand with the hoeing" Dad said, fed up with the ball kicking.

"He doesn't like me to help him", replied John, with a quick excuse.

"That's because you don't help him properly. If you put your back into it like you do with sport it would be much better. And you, Constantin, you can clean out the stables".

"But Dad, that's a rotten job and it stinks. I don't like doing it," complained the boy.

"Who on earth does?" replied Dad, "But all of us have to do things we don't like at times. Perhaps Basil will help you".

"No, he won't, you know he's always around Mum's skirts".

With a great lack of enthusiasm John picked up a hoe and headed slowly for the fields, while Constantin disappeared into the barn. I knew where I'd find him later, he'd be stuck in the corner of the hay loft with his nose in a book.

Anyone could see the two brothers felt unhappy about working on the farm during their holidays, but when John complained to Mum that it was unfair to have to help on the farm while his fellow students living in the town were not expected to do anything but play, Mum strongly disagreed. "You should be happy to help your father when you can. He works so hard just to keep you in college and if he could not afford it, you'd be working all the time on the farm, so I want to hear no more complaints about that!"

However, the holidays brought a different atmosphere to the farm. With all of us at home there was so much animation and high spirits. Meal times were filled with excited chatter. John and Constantin introduced us to new games. From somewhere they had acquired a bicycle, a bit of an old boneshaker, but for me to sit on the crossbar with one of my brothers riding us round the village was just the greatest treat.

When the summer holidays ended and the boys returned to college, Mary and I missed their companionship very much indeed, perhaps Sanda even more so. She was now six and becoming quite pretty, with her long blonde hair and blue eyes. She was still Mum's darling at home, and the boys spoiled her outrageously, always giving her a little more of any treat than either Mary or me. I myself felt protective about her, and as she grew older we became closer together, and later were as inseparable as John and Constantin.

Autumn soon came, and with it the scent of pickling vegetables and the sharp tang of boiling vinegar permeated the air of the village. Mum spent hours in the kitchen preparing all the produce for pickling, with Mary and I washing hundreds of cucumbers, tomatoes and peppers, while Dad arranged them in special barrels before pouring on the boiling liquids. The activity was hectic, but so very rewarding as the jars were filled and placed in orderly rows on the cellar shelves, and the filled barrels rolled carefully into place.

In the fields people were busy harvesting, with the families helping each other to bring in the crops. When all the village had cut and stacked the cereals came the time for the threshing to start. Some of the smaller holdings threshed in the ancient way by hand, or by walking the horse over the sheaves, but all the larger farms had to arrange for the owner of the threshing machine to come to them. It was one of the few oil driven machines to be seen in the village, and for many days its loud putt-putt was heard, with the tell-tale plume of bluish smoke hanging about over the farms. This was another time for mutual help, for it needed up to fifteen people to run the threshing. One sat on top cutting the ties of the sheaves and feeding the machine, others cleared the chaff, bagged the grain, stacked the straw, carried sheaves to the machine and, hardest of all, tossed the sheaves to the top man with the aid of a pitchfork. Dad's job was to stand by the scale to see how many kilos had been bagged and to supervise the whole operation, while Mum was busy feeding all the workers. It was her pride to feed them well but it meant so much cooking that she had to ask her sisters or Marika to give her a hand in the kitchen.

For meals, everyone came in covered in dust, and Mary and I worked hard keeping the washing troughs filled with water and handing out towels and soap. We also helped put out the dishes of food, which meant I had many an odd snack on the way.

Then came the grape picking, when the vineyard was filled with activity, joy and laughter. How many grapes I put into the big baskets is beyond measure, but I do know a great many found their way into my mouth.

Dad and Ephraim set up the great wood and iron press in the yard, and as the fruit arrived by the cartful it was fed into the machine. Every turn of the thick iron handle on the screw squeezed out the purple juice into the collection tray to be funnelled into the waiting barrels. I was always hanging about the press as were the others, waiting hopefully for Mum to give us glasses of the sweet liquid. The juice left each of us youngsters with purple moustaches, which I thought great fun. We had much competition from the wasps and bees attracted by the scent of the grapes but they were regarded as part of the scene and did not worry us.

The cellar soon began to fill with huge barrels of wine as well as the smaller casks of pickles. On the stone shelves stood pots of aubergines and peppers, bottles of sweet fruit juices, jars of peaches and apricots and on each side of the steps other jars filled with honey. I loved the mixture of so many scents, all combined with the slight mouldy smell of dampness from the sand and earth floor, so thickening the air it almost had substance.

Mum and Dad always felt relaxed once the harvest was over, the fields ploughed, the cellar full and the animals bedded down for winter.

Now was the time for the second windows to be fixed to the inside of the frames, but before this was done Mum made little artificial flowers from paper and cotton wool to sit on the sill between the two panes of glass so that we had something colourful to look at when all outside was white. Once the cold weather came, and with it the snow, the farm was soon covered in a thick white blanket while Jack Frost drew his intricate patterns of ice crystals over the windows.

Dad and Ephraim, with less to do, spent their time feeding the animals, cleaning and repairing the equipment and harness, keeping the paths, doors and barns clear of snow. Mum concentrated on the indoor tasks of weaving and mending clothes, together, of course, with the unending chores of cooking, cleaning and washing.

It was the time when all the materials for the household were made, most of them by Mum, but it was also the time when she called in Mania, a woman in the village who was famed for making the most beautiful carpets for hanging on the walls or for the floors. She was unfortunately handicapped by having a wooden leg. Not a sophisticated articulating false limb, but merely a wooden peg which strapped to her stump. She was a serious hard working woman who loved her craft. Unmarried and with no family, she seemed as happy to work for us as Mum was to have her do so. She lived in during the winter time and I think she loved to stay with us, such a large family with so many children around making fun and treating her as a member of the household, for otherwise life in her tiny cottage was very lonely.

The wooden leg must have been quite an uncomfortable appliance, for when she was weaving she would remove the peg and put it to one side. Naturally John and Constantin, when on holiday, could never resist making a game of it, and they, at times, stole away with the leg and hid it. Mania, wanting to move and finding the peg missing, realised it was the boys again. Always good humoured about it, she said, in pretended rage "Come on, you devils, give me back my leg, so that I can give you a good thump with my crutch!"

I was most intrigued by the way she could look at a roughly drawn pattern fixed to the side of the frame, and translate it into an intricate coloured carpet, with all the pieces of wool being put into the weaving at exactly the right time and in the correct position. Together with my two sisters I spent hours watching the picture take shape. The designs were those which had been handed down from generation to generation, traditional to Bessarabia. Usually they have a central motif of a boy and a girl holding bunches of flowers, a pair of butterflies, two peacocks or two angels, all in pleasant warm colours, on a black background, with a border of interwoven flowers.

At this time of year I was happy to see much more of Mum and

Dad, for they were able to take life easier without working in the fields all hours.

Mum had the loom set up in the house and whenever she had spare time she would weave some cotton or linen cloth, singing as she worked to the clacking rhythm of the shuttles. I crept often into the room and watched her cheerfully working away on some material. I listened enraptured to the folksongs she sang in her soft tuneful voice. If she saw me she stopped, lifted me up on her lap and tried to show me how to operate the pedals, but my legs were not long enough to reach them.

"See what I am weaving now, Lia? Your Mum will make this into a bedspread for Mary's bottom drawer, and next year I'll make one for you!"

In this farm we were nearer to George's family and saw them more often. Marika's father, who we called *Cuscru*, was a bluff good humoured man, very tall and well built, with a large stomach protruding over his thick leather belt. His jolly round face had laughing eyes which always seemed a-twinkle. When the snow was thick and fresh, he came to our house with his large sleigh, pulled by two horses. The dog barked dementedly and I looked out to see this big man, clad in his thick sheep-skin jacket and fur hat, lead his horses into the yard. "Nicola!" he shouted, with a great guffaw, "I've come to take your children away!" We knew then that he was to take us out on the sleigh.

After the fuss of greetings, Mum dressed us all in warm clothes, settled us on the sledge, covered us with blankets and admonished us to be good. Then Marika's father mounted the driving seat, cracked his whip, and we were away. The horses had bells hung around their necks, which tinkled a silvery sound out across the snow laden fields. The runners hissed through the crisp flakes and the hooves of the horses thudded ahead, muffled on the soft carpet. All about us the virgin whiteness was deep and unmarked, the cold icy air stung our cheeks as we rushed along at a great pace. The roofs of the houses gleamed cream and gold in the brilliance of the winter sun, the trees sparkled and glittered with their arms full of frost and ice diamonds. Great ghostly clouds of vapour rose from the nostrils of the labouring horses to evaporate in the still air. It was as a fairy story for me, so romantic a time and place. What more could I ever dream of, so beautiful, so peaceful, so happy! To add to my overflowing enjoyment Marika's father laughed and joked and teased us with nonsense riddles. Our trips in the sleigh lasted an hour or two before we returned home.

"Nicola, I've brought your chicks all back safe and sound. What a wonderful ride I've had with them, but now I'd better get back as my other half will want me to do some work".

"Don't go yet, *Cuscru*, there's some hot wine here to warm you", said Dad, pouring out glasses of the steaming hot cinnamon spiced wine.

"You are so lucky, you and Nicola, to have so many lovely kids, I've only Marika".

"I think you are probably the lucky one", replied Dad, not meaning a word of it, "look at the way I have to work to keep them all fed and clothed!"

"I know you wouldn't change it even if you could, would he Nicola?" asked *Cuscru*, turning to Mum for confirmation.

"He would not, that's for sure, the kids are his pride and joy".

"If the weather lasts I'll take them out again when I get the chance, it's better than sitting on my bottom arguing with Natalie".

We were given little sips of the hot wine, which made us feel very grown up, and we waited eagerly for our next sleigh ride.

Then, in mid winter, Christmas came, with all its attendant preparations and excitements. Mum fattened the turkey with maize, Dad called in someone to slaughter the pig. This was the part I disliked greatly, and would go away so as not to see the animal killed. Once done the carcass was turned over a straw fire to singe off the bristles. Dad rubbed it all over with maize flour to clean the burnt residue and Mum cut and sorted the meat for its various uses. Back legs for hams, hung in a special alcove in the chimney to smoke. From the poorer cuts she made sausages and brawn, with the trotters supplying the gelatine. The best pieces she fried and stored in large pots filled afterwards with melted fat. These stayed preserved for months in the cool cellar.

In addition to the meats there was the *cozonac* of which Mum made at least a dozen, for we were a large family and many visitors came to us over the Christmas period. I loved watching Mum make the cakes, we children especially liked the ones filled with ground walnuts, sugar and cocoa.

"If you want walnut cake you must crack and clean the nuts for me", said Mum, in reply to our many requests. Basil smashed the nuts with a big stone, and Mary and I separated the shells from the kernels. What we did not eat on the spot went into the cakes.

There were traditions other than the food which excited me. I loved the groups of carol singers who came before Christmas, the little boys dressed in thick coats and huge lambswool hats which obliterated from view all but their red noses. They came into the courtyard and asked.

"May we sing carols for you?" Mum and Dad never refused the singers, who began by ringing handbells and, at each pause in the singing, ringing them again. We crowded at the door, listening to the traditional old songs of the coming of Jesus. I felt very emotional, with tears not far away, at the stories of love and devotion. When they finished their repertoire Mum offered them specially made pretzel rings and walnuts. Some of the singers carried hooked sticks on which they slipped the rings, often collecting twenty or more from various houses.

The great day came. Usually for dinner we had pork, turkey, chicken in aspic and specially made sausages, followed by *sarmale* (meat and rice balls in cabbage leaves) and, of course, *cozonac*. It was such a feast after the meat free days of advent.

In the evening Mum and Dad gathered us all round the ikon, lit a candle beneath and sang carols and hymns in praise of our Lord. The boys joined in, their younger voices blending with the adults. The atmosphere was so spiritual and magical my heart overflowed with the beauty of that moment, with its message of peace and goodwill.

I felt so safe and sure in that friendly house, with all my family surrounding me. Little did I know that the Christmas of 1939 would be the last one we should ever celebrate together like this.

The first day of Christmas was always a day for the family but the next two days were given over to visits. Mum dressed us in our best, and off we went to pay our respects to our various grannies, grandads, uncles and aunts. As Dad had four sisters and Mum three sisters and a brother, there were quite a few relatives to see. The snow was often thick and we younger ones had to struggle to make headway with heavy boots on our short legs.

Quickly on the heels of Christmas came the New Year, another feast. I liked this day, it wasn't as serious as Christmas. In the morning a group of youngsters came to each house with a pair of oxen pulling a plough which was decorated with paper flowers and ribbons. They had a peculiar musical instrument with them made from a skin stretched over a barrel, with a tuft of hair attached to the skin. Pulling the hair made a deep booming bull like noise. They also had bells to ring and whips to crack. They shouted out phrases and rhymes wishing everyone good health and a good crop for the coming year. The group went from house to house repeating their goodwill message.

I also liked the tradition of the *sorcova*. This was a stick adorned with artificial flowers and ribbons. Children visited their nearest relatives and tapped them with the *sorcova* while repeating the rhyme:

> "*May you live and flourish*
> *As an apple tree in summer,*
> *Strong as iron,*
> *Fast as an arrow,*
> *For the coming year,*
> *And many more to follow*"

This was supposed to charm in good luck for the following year, but 1940 was to be a year of sorrow and suffering for my family, and to change our lives completely.

THREE

Life in our village flew past in this normal happy way until the summer. There had been vague talk of a war in western Europe since 1939 but it seemed very remote from the people living in such a tranquil village. My parents were not to know yet of the political moves taking place in the background which would radically alter our lives.

The war burst into flame in May 1940 with the German invasion of France and by June the twenty second the fighting was virtually over as France capitulated. On June twenty seventh of that year, the Romanian government, by then pro-fascist, was forced by Hitler to hand Bessarabia over to Russia. Within days Russian paratroops landed along the new frontier of the river Prut and effectively sealed our region off from the rest of Romania.

Although my parents avoided talking about such events in front of us little girls, we inevitably picked up some of the bad news from the other children at school.

Shortly after the Russians occupied us many monstrous changes were made in the laws and the system of government.

I was then too young to understand and be afraid of words like occupation, communism, Stalinism and bolsheviks, but I did notice that Mum and Dad now often had worried faces and whispered to each other so that we should not hear their conversation. A lot of the gaiety had gone from Mum's demeanour.

It was strange, in our highly religious community, to hear that the bolsheviks did not believe in God, and that in Russia the churches had been closed or turned into stables. Everybody was afraid that all the land would now be taken from the peasants and joined into collectives as in Russia, when all would work for no reward except a meal from the communal bowl. To our small village these were terrifying rumours, and the atmosphere of happiness and security which had been with us so shortly before quickly changed to one of worry and despondency. Dark clouds slowly descended on our peaceful farm.

Although I am sure my parents were aware that under the Russian occupation the richer farmers might suffer they refused to accept that anything terrible could happen to them and apparently went about their normal labour. It was as if life carried on in a strange sort of void, everyone waiting with dread for something to happen, but without knowing quite what.

As far as I know no Russians came to stay in our village but we soon heard that the mayor in Kiperceni had been replaced and new communist officials were running the administration.

Less than two months after the occupation, just as harvest was coming to its peak, a man arrived on horseback at the farm, asking for Dad, who was out in the fields. The horseman gave Mum a message that Dad had to go urgently to the regional soviet office in Kiperceni. Mum, flustered by this sudden call, sent Basil to find Dad and bring him home. I remember how tired and worried he looked when he came in. He took off his sweat stained clothes and washed while Mum brought him some fresh things. When dressed and ready to go Mum bade him wait a little, while she brought him a comb to tidy his hair. "Oh, forget it Nicola", he said, on the way to the gate, "I'm only off to see one of these new bosses, I'm not going courting!"

"Will you take one of the horses?"

"No, they are all being worked in the fields, perhaps a passing cart will give me a lift". He set off to walk the few kilometers to Kiperceni.

After Dad left, Mum continued with her chores, slightly worried as to what could be so urgent for him, but not unduly disturbed because so many changes were being made. It was probably something to do with that.

However time passed and it began to get dark. Dad still had not returned and Mum began to show signs of apprehension. At dinner all of us children sat around the table, but our appetites had vanished, sensing Mum's mood and fearing something was amiss. She ate nothing, but fidgetted and fussed about us. "Where on earth can that man be? Why doesn't he come home? It's dark now and the office must have closed ages ago!"

"He's probably met someone on the way home and called in for a glass of wine and a chat", said John, trying to calm her fears, but without much success.

We stayed late, sitting by the table, mostly silent, consumed with some indefinable inner dread. As there was no sign of Dad returning we younger ones were sent to bed while Mum cleared up.

When I awoke next morning only Mary and Sanda were in the house.

"Did Dad come home?" I asked Mary. "No", she replied, "Mum sent John and Constantin to Kiperceni to look for him, and she went out to help Ephraim with the harvest".

It was late afternoon before Mum returned, hot, tired and obviously worried.

"Are the boys home yet?"

"No, not yet Mum", answered Mary. Upset, Mum went to wash while I played with Sanda in the yard, then she sat on the cool verandah, resting.

The moment we heard the sound of the gate opening she rushed out to confront the boys.

"Where is your father? What's happened to him?" John, his face unusually pale, began to mumble hesitantly as though it was difficult for him to speak.

"What happened?" repeated Mum, almost shouting. She took hold of John by the shoulders and shook him.

"Tell me, tell me, what's happened to your father?"

John drew a deep breath and in a rush of words burst out.

"He's being held for interrogation in the NKVD office". Mum paused for a moment then said loudly. "Interrogation, what do you mean, interrogation? He's a good man, he's never done anything wrong. Why is he being interrogated?" She continued asking for several minutes. John, receiving the brunt of her diatribe, could only shrug his shoulders hopelessly. Mum repeated the same questions over and over again, becoming almost hysterical, speaking incoherently and I thought she was going mad. I stood rooted to the spot, looking at her, listening to words which sounded strange. I did not understand them. Then she suddenly collapsed heavily, slumping on the steps. John came close to her and held her gently. "We've got to go back tomorrow, we can see him then". Mum seemed not to hear. She dragged herself upright, went into the house, knelt before the ikon and began to pray. Confused and disturbed I crept into the room behind her and cried. The rest of the evening passed miserably, mostly in silence, with none of us understanding the reason for Dad's detention.

Next day, as I later heard from Basil, John and Constantin went to the NKVD where, after waiting some time in a small corridor, Dad was brought out by a policeman. He looked drawn, haggard and exhausted. With trembling hands he snatched his two sons close to him and hugged them tightly. Tears glistened in his eyes as he said.

"They are going to send me to the prison in Orhei. I don't know why, no one will tell me anything".

At that point the guard interrupted abruptly. "That's all, visiting time is finished", then he pushed Dad roughly back towards the door. While being forced along he shouted.

"John, please bring my sheepskin jacket tomorrow. It's cold here at night and I have nothing to cover myself with. Don't let Mum come, I'm worried how she would react to seeing me in this place!"

The following day all three brothers (for Basil had insisted on joining the other two) walked again to the NKVD. They arrived just in time to see father, together with a few other men, being herded into a motor van.

"Wait a minute, wait a minute!" screamed John at the police who were standing by the vehicle. "I want to give this jacket to my father!" One of the guards snatched the proffered jacket from the boy and threw it to Dad, without allowing him to say goodbye to his sons, pushing him instead into the van with unnecessary force. Once the prisoners were inside, the doors were slammed shut, cutting father off from the sight of his boys. As the van moved away, Basil ran after it in a vain attempt to climb aboard. He was calling out in his anguish, "Dad, Dad, where are they taking you, what can we do without you?"

The only reply he received was the cloud of dust as the vehicle gathered speed, shortly to turn a corner and vanish from view. The three sons were left in a dejected little group, staring towards the direction in which the van had gone, taking their dear father further away from them every minute.

When they returned home from Kiperceni John sighed a deep sigh before telling Mum that they had seen father being taken to the prison. Shocked at such bad news she clutched at her throat, gasping for breath, almost on the point of fainting, her face a ghastly ashen colour as she struggled to regain her breath and her composure. She leaned back against the fence for support. Alarmed at her reaction Basil ran to fetch Auntie Alexandra. By the time they both reached the house Mum, helped by John, had gone inside, with us following. She knelt at the ikon and prayed aloud in her anguish. "God almighty, help me. Don't leave me here alone with so many children and so much to do. I cannot face all the demands by these evil bolsheviks. Bring Theodore back, please God, why punish me so hard?"

Auntie hurried to Mum, almost on the point of collapse again and now in floods of tears. Holding her close Auntie tried to console her. "It must be some stupid mistake. He'll be back soon, I'm sure". Then turning to us, said softly. "Go out and play, all of you, don't bother your mum just now". We slowly and reluctantly obeyed her, not wanting to play, not understanding why Father was taken from us. This was our first contact with the terror and cruelty of the Russian occupation.

In the days which followed I felt so unhappy and wretched. Every evening I waited for Dad to return and hold me on his knee with his strong arm about me. I could not make any sense of what had happened. The feeling of unbearable loss and emptiness did not diminish with the passing of time. Mum was blaming herself and feeling guilty at not foreseeing the gravity of Dad's situation and insisting on going to see him.

How terribly sad was the first Sunday without Dad when we

dressed to go to church. People looked at us with sympathy, several women asking Mum questions.

Once inside I turned my head frequently towards the place where Father should have been, but the boys stood there alone. I glanced at the altar which he usually faced and asked myself why did God take him away from us? How had he sinned so greatly? From that day on Sunday had much less significance for me, despite Mum's efforts to keep it as before.

In autumn the boys returned to college and I once again resumed school. Life went on somehow with the same sort of routine as before, but the atmosphere had changed dramatically, with Mum being sad and worried the whole time, knowing absolutely nothing about father's plight.

Awful stories of people, even whole families, being arrested and sent to Siberia began to circulate through the village. In spite of these rumours we all still refused to think Dad would be deported to such a place, of which I knew nothing except that it was a dreadful region very far away.

After a while I started reluctantly to accept Dad's absence, but I still hoped each day that by some miracle I would find him there when I returned from school. I was very miserable to see Mum so exhausted and different. She became more and more irritable and short-tempered as never before. Young as I was I could not make easily the connection between her changed ways and Dad's continued absence.

As the weeks passed Mum found it increasingly difficult to run the farm with any efficiency, for in addition to normal work in the fields she had to cope with the local authorities demands for her to take one of our carts to load and carry stone to a nearby roadworks. She tried to send Ephraim in her place, but he came back having been told that *she* had to do the work, not him. Nothing was paid for this at all.

Then, shortly afterwards, the authorities ordered Mum to use two carts to carry stone. Obviously she could not drive both at the same time and she was then forced to take Ephraim to help. This meant that the fields became neglected and full of weeds. As well as this, quotas of produce were now demanded from all farms. These were specially made higher for Mum, so high as to be impossible to fulfill, forcing her to buy produce to meet the targets set. She tried very hard to employ some people to work on the farm but with little success, as the propaganda of the new regime, of equality for all, caught the imagination of the poorer people who had originally worked for others. Many of them feared that if they worked for *Kulaks* (rich farmers) they would also be deported. The only help Mum had, apart from Ephraim, was from George and her brothers-in-law, who came sporadically and with great effort, for they all had their own farms to run.

A seemingly obvious way for her to ease the burden would have been to sell some land, but this now proved impossible as everyone expected that at some future time all land would be confiscated by the state and turned into collectives. Worry and tension now showed on Mum's face all the time, and were reflected in her person, as she became noticeably thinner. She badly needed the boys at home to help her, but despite all her trouble she was still determined to not give up their college education, which for her was more important than anything else.

Another shock was yet to come. The priest, whom Mum had badgered often to get news of Father, came to our house bringing the terrible tidings that he had been deported to Siberia for five years imprisonment.

For days Mum was sick and ill with the trauma of this news and took to her bed while Auntie Alexandra, Mum's closest sister, and Marika took care of her and us. As soon as we were home from school Basil, Mary and I, together with Sanda, stayed by her bed, kissing and touching her, cuddling up to her and telling all that we had done that day. She forced herself to smile at us and I think we helped her gain the strength to recover. She now seemed to find comfort in having one or other of us girls sleeping with her. On these nights if I awoke and accidentally touched her cheeks I often found them wet with tears. On many occasions, entering the kitchen, I caught her wiping her eyes, but forcing a smile for me.

She was now working so hard she came into the house completely drained. Often she fell asleep while eating her meal. In spite of this there never passed a night when, before going to bed, she would not light the little votive lamp beneath the ikon, fall on her knees and pray for Dad's health and safe return to us. She was frequently in tears as she prayed, while we stayed as silent sad shadows in the background. After she knew that Dad had been sent to Siberia she must have lived in constant fear of herself being deported.

From now on whenever the boys were on holiday at home they worked full time on the farm. I suppose neither of them was happy with their hard lot, for instead of being out with the village lads they spent the hours weeding, hoeing or stacking hay. But it was bearable for them knowing how much Mum appreciated and relied on their help. None of us could add to Mum's sorrow, we loved her too much and now she was the only one left to love.

Then one day Ephraim, Mum's mainstay on the farm, threw her a bombshell by announcing that he was going to marry. This upset Mum greatly, not because of the marriage as such, or any dislike of the future daughter-in-law, but because she would be losing her greatest help, the only one capable of doing a man's job and coping with the farming problems.

However, Auntie Alexandra had a different point of view on the matter. "It's not time to despair, Nicola, for you can give him ten hectares of land. That means you'll have less taxes to pay, less quotas to find and less land to work. In these days, as you well know, it's no good to have too much property".

The wedding was quite a sober affair, with no great traditional feast, for most of the people were so generally depressed with the current situation that no one had any heart for a big festival. There was a small gathering in Kiperceni from which we girls were excluded, and the first time I really knew there had been a wedding was when Ephraim brought home a very pretty girl in a flowered dress.

"This is Ileana", he said, happily introducing his bride to Sanda and me. "From tomorrow she will live here with us until we move into the old farm by the river".

I liked Ileana right away for her wide dimpled smile. I heard from John that she was only nineteen, and from quite a rich family. She had two sisters and a brother, younger than her. Mum was pleased to have her with us as her cheerfulness came like a ray of sunshine into our farm, which for these summer months had seemed so miserable and dull. She had rosy cheeks and radiated happiness, often singing as she worked, as Mum herself had previously done. She had a straight backed sylph like figure, with a wide innocent face, which was misleading to those unprepared for her direct manner of speech. Anyone Ileana did not like was left in no doubt about her feelings.

The young couple stayed with us for only a short time, a few weeks, until one Sunday Ephraim packed his belongings, wedding gifts and bride into one of the carts, harnessed to a pair of draught cattle which had been given by Mum as a dowry, and, with a flick of the whip, drove away to their new life, leaving us yet more sad that another member of the family had left home.

Less than a month later, Ileana came bursting into the yard, breathless, flushed and quite distraught. She ran to Mum who was in the barn, embraced her tightly, her eyes running with tears.

"Whatever is the matter?" asked Mum in alarm. "What's happened, have you and Ephraim had an argument?"

"No, no", sobbed Ileana, "Nothing like that". She continued, forcing her words out between clenched teeth. "I went to visit mother and father but couldn't find them. I couldn't find anyone about the place, so searched all round. There was no one, not Serafima or Vera or John. They weren't in the fields either. Then I saw Auntie Irena and she said that yesterday", and here she broke off into a renewed bout of sobbing before continuing, agony in her voice, "yesterday the police turned up with two motor vans and took them all away, all of them, mother and my two sisters in one van, and father and John in the other, God knows why". She paused for a moment. "You don't think they'll be sent to that Siberian hell, do you?" There was pleading in her voice.

"I don't know love, I just don't know any more what to think", said Mum.

"God curse these wretched Bolshevik swine, all they ever do is spread evil". Ileana spat out the last sentence vehemenently before lapsing into another bout of weeping, holding tightly to the older woman. Mum slowly walked her into the house, away from my sharp little ears.

I was so upset by this scene that I went and sat on the verandah, myself on the verge of tears. Into my mind came the images of the happy pretty faces of Ileana's sisters, when I had last seen them, on a visit to their house after the wedding. Now all I could think of was of them shut in some dark windowless van, to be taken somewhere into the unknown, seemingly without rhyme or reason. How frightened they must be! What could they possibly have done to deserve this? Life seemed to be turning into some sort of nightmare.

These latest terrible tidings made me think again of my father. Where was he and what was happening to him? How I missed him, with his cheerful word to the horses in the morning and his kisses and embraces for us when the workday ended. It was worse on Sunday, going to the church without him, no longer being able to climb on his knee after lunch, to be held so caringly.

Then Sanda, who had been somewhere else in the yard when Ileana arrived, came running along wanting me to join in some game or other she had invented. I left the verandah and my black mood slowly evaporated.

Winter that year brought Mum even greater hardship, for only us three girls were at home, Basil having gone to the school in Orhei. Ephraim lived in the other house and had his own piece of land, leaving almost the whole of the work burden on Mum's shoulders.

There was a brief period of happiness when Christmas came and brought us all together, with the added bonus of the strong young arms of John, Constantin and Basil tackling some of the outstanding jobs which would surely have overwhelmed Mum but for the loyalty of Toma Beiu, who had worked for Dad and came from time to time to deal with some of the heavier tasks. George and Ephraim helped as often as possible but much had to be left undone.

The quotas imposed by the local authority were continuously and deliberately increased to a point when Mum found it utterly impossible to fulfil them any longer, in spite of mustering all the help she could. Most of the farm remained neglected with the lack of labour.

Consequently, in June 1941, less than a year after Father had been whisked away, Mum received a summons to go to the NKVD office in Kiperceni. Before she set off she hugged and kissed us girls a few times, then crossed the fields to see the boys who, being at the beginning of their summer holidays, were now working on the farm. I had the feeling that something was wrong, as she never usually made that much fuss when she was going out. It was the last I saw of Mum.

We waited and waited for her to return, but to no avail. For much of the time there was a whispered conversation going on between John and Constantin, who were using strange, unusual words which had little meaning for me. A black dread gripped my soul and I feared she would, like Father, never come back home. Yet she had to. How could we survive without her? Thinking about losing Mum was just too much to bear. I went to bed and cried until sleep, at long last, took over and silenced me.

The next day all three brothers walked into Kiperceni as they had done when Father had been called to the office, leaving us with Auntie Alexandra.

After what seemed to be forever they returned and Mary and I pounced on them with questions. "Where's Mum? Why isn't she with you? When is she coming home? Sanda began to cry. John put his arm round her and said gently, "Come, my little sister, we'll go to the kitchen and find something nice for you", and took her away from us.

Left with Constantin, who looked pale and ill, we repeated the same questions. He did not answer us, but after pausing for a while said, in a trembling voice, "I want you to say a prayer with me for our *Mama* as she may not be back for some time".

He embraced us both tightly and tried not to cry, but the tears came, as they did with Mary and me.

I was utterly shocked by the news Constantin had brought, that Mum would not come back. I felt as though I did not want to live, so many awful things were happening, but I had no idea how to die. "Mum," I whispered through my tears, "please come back, come home to us!"

I hoped that she would be away just a short time, as Constantin said, but in my heart I knew it would not be. Rubbing my face while the tears still poured from my eyes, I asked helplessly, "What'll we do without Mum? What can we do without her?"

That day I wandered about aimlessly or sat on the verandah looking into space, bursting into intermittent spells of weeping. Next to me stood Mary, the tears running down her face as they were down mine. We held on to each other and cried together, having lost the two beings most precious to us, our dear Mum and Dad. Mum had always been there, loving, caring and advising. What could I do now, any of us do, without her? Sanda, Mum's blonde little angel with the big blue eyes, just followed me around like a pathetic lost puppy. Again and again I asked myself why this should happen to my parents, and who were these monsters who had stolen them from me.

It was not until later that I learned the brothers had seen Mum in Kiperceni and found her red eyed with weeping and quite devastated. She hugged and kissed them many times. With some difficulty in speaking at such an emotional time she managed to tell them the terrible news that she was to be sent to the prison in Orhei, and asked them to bring her a quilt the following day. She pleaded with them to be kind and take care of us girls, hoping she would only be away a little while.

The boys returned to her the next day with the quilt. There was a heartbreaking parting, with Mum eventually being forced from them by the unfeeling guards. The three of them were shattered by the separation, Basil worse of all as he had been so close to Mother, who had meant everything to him.

I was often kept awake at nights wondering what would become of us. If I fell asleep I had such bad dreams of my brothers being taken away one by one, of Sanda crying so much about Mum that she became ill, of myself being locked in a dark and freezing cellar screaming for help.

It was such a relief for the daylight to come and banish the nightmare hours of darkness.

Left on our own we were completely shattered and disorientated. Our stability and security had suddenly been snatched from us. For days we drifted about in limbo, with no proper meals, no fresh clothes, just confusion. Sanda hid away often in a corner and cried, suffering the shock of Mum's disappearance.

It was normal at such a time that we should turn to our relatives for help and reassurance and Auntie Alexandra, Marika and George came often to see that we were eating something, trying to give us comfort. Marika was so affectionate and not afraid of showing her feelings, and at the time I found John's jocular nature a welcome relief. As to what was to be done with us, John and Constantin decided that it would be better to remain together on the farm during the summer holidays, but Mary, Sanda and I should move in with some relatives when school started again.

"In that case you must look after yourselves more sensibly than you are doing now", George said.

We had only had one decent meal for the past week, and that had been cooked by Marika. For the rest of the time we had munched bread, walnuts, cheese and honey. Luckily there was plenty of milk from the cow.

The morning after it had been decided that we should remain in the house for the holiday, we were awakened by George. It was quite late and we all had been sound asleep. He shook the boys roughly until they opened their eyes.

"Get up", he ordered brusquely, "Is this how you look after yourselves? Sleeping late, no animals fed, nothing done at all? The cow is distressed and needs milking. You had better start doing something otherwise you'll have to be split up amongst the relatives".

The boys roused themselves shamefacedly and dressed. Previously Mum and Dad had seen to everything and I had no idea how much there was to do. Now I began to find out that nothing was done by magic. We all were beginning to learn some very hard lessons. Marika next spurred us girls into getting some order into our lives. She brought along a large bowl of dough for us to bake for bread, coming into the house early enough to catch us in all sorts and stages of dress, eating bread and walnuts for breakfast.

"My God", she greeted us, "You kids stink. Are these the same clothes you've been wearing since your mum went?" We admitted they were but hadn't thought too much about it.

"Well, just look at you, whatever would Mum think if she came through that door now? She would really be ashamed of you". She paused, looking at us thoughfully, then continued, "Mary, you are the oldest, make sure all of you change your clothes. Then you'll have to wash them. Basil can carry the water and wood, and see to the fire. It's no good moping about all day! Start getting things done and you'll have more to think about!"

Marika was right. Once we started to work we had a lot less time to brood over our troubles. I became quite tired for there was little time for relaxation or play now, the simplest things Mum had taken in her stride took us so much longer and were not done very well. Many mistakes were made, of course, as when Mary put the tins of dough that Marika had brought into the oven, forgot about it while doing something else until the smell of burning reminded her, then found the oven full of blackened crusts. After this Marika let us make the dough ourselves, a hard job for our small hands, but it made sure that no more bread was burnt.

By the time harvest came things were more or less under control. Mary prepared simple meals; soups, stews, salads or pastas and there was always fruit in plenty at this time of year. We still had enough stores of basic foods like flour and grain, cheese, honey and preserves and many eggs. For fresh meat we had the chickens, ducks, geese and sometimes pork. The garden provided masses of vegetables.

But the life without Mum and Dad was very hard. I had bouts of frustrated weeping at times when I was up against some difficulty I could not solve, or when Sanda asked when Mum would be back. Some days seemed so overwhelmingly black. If I hurt myself I automatically looked around for Mum, until the fact hit me like a blow in the face that there was no Mum any more. I cried over the silliest thing, and often begged God to bring her back soon, then I could ask her all about whatever troubled me.

Basil, Mary and even Sanda grew much more mature in those few weeks. Mary was gradually taking over Mum's role. To my eyes she changed from a bossy rather irritating girl to a warm helpful sister, certainly becoming more conscientious than the two older brothers who, considering their days work in the fields was enough for their share, would argue over whether they should fetch water or carry wood. This often reduced Mary to tears for she had to rely on their strength for some heavy jobs. I think we all gave Mary a hard time, which was quite unfair as she was only eleven.

One task beyond us all was bringing in the harvest, but George solved it neatly by suggesting that we should give half of the produce to anyone who would do the work for us. There were plenty of volunteers at that price and the crops were brought in, enabling us to replenish some of our stocks for the following year. The grape harvest did not bother us as George was the winemaker and he and Ephraim would see to that after we returned to school.

As to what was happening outside our village I had little idea. At times the boys spoke with George about the German advance and the Russian retreat but it did not mean much to me. Romania was now in the war on the side of the Germans who had been fighting the Russians since the twenty second of June 1941. Then we heard the almost unbelievable news that the Russians had fled from Kiperceni and Orhei. Right away John and Constantin hurried to the prison to look for Mum. After walking the sixteen kilometres to the town and spending some hours there, the two brothers returned with a terrible story.

When they arrived at the prison the gates were open and the building apparently abandoned, so summoning up their courage they entered. There was no one in the place, but in one of the courtyards they saw great gaps and holes in the walls, with cartridge cases littering the ground and a great deal of bloodstained concrete. Venturing further into the building despite an awful smell, they found that bodies had been piled in some of the cells. Shocked at this sight they hurriedly retreated.

In the town they were told that when the Russians had left, in a great panic, they had lined up and shot all the remaining prisoners. These unfortunates were the latest arrivals. All prisoners who had been taken at the same time as Mum had already been sent to Siberia.

To me it sounded so horrible and ghastly. As the only dead person I had seen was my grandad, who just looked as though he was asleep, I could not imagine the sight my brothers were describing. I was so upset Mum had been sent to Siberia I could not stop crying, but John lifted me up and hugged me. "Don't cry, Lia, we must thank God that she escaped this massacre, and pray for her safety wherever she is."

My first glimpse of anything warlike was when Ephraim came into the yard one day dressed as a soldier.

Once the Russians had withdrawn from Bessarabia, retreating before the Germans, the Romanian army had re-entered our region and the young men were being conscripted. Ephraim was one of them.

The next sign of war was a great deal more dramatic than Ephraim in his uniform. One day, while Mary and I were in the summer kitchen preparing dinner, with Sanda standing close by, we became conscious of the noise of heavy machines getting ever nearer. Basil rushed out of the gate to investigate and returned breathless.

"The Germans are coming here!" he gasped.

We had hardly time to absorb this fact when there was the louder noise of a lorry in the lane and moments later, amid shouting, the gates of the yard were thrust open with considerable force. As the three of us watched, afraid but curious, a covered lorry tried to back into the yard. This was not possible because the wooden roof over the gates was too low. More shouting followed, then, to our consternation, three soldiers in grey uniforms, with long shiny boots and peaked caps, pistols in their belts, strode in. We ducked out of sight behind the curtains, peeping through the window. At the sound of these men, speaking in a strange language, John came from one of the barns and tried to talk to them.

"I think John's been learning German at college" whispered Mary.

With many hand gestures to make up for his lack of words John eventually got their message, descending into the cellar and returning with a jug of wine. Then he entered the house and brought out a plate of bread and cheese. The soldiers sat on the steps of the house, taking great gulps of the wine in turn and eating the food.

After a short while, one who seemed to be in charge stood up with the jug in his hands and asked John to refill it. We girls still stayed low. Minutes later Basil, who appeared from the garden, was sent by John to the barn, to return with a small basket of eggs. One soldier took two, cracked them and swallowed them raw.

From the moment the gates had opened, Bob had been barking loudly, running up and down his length of wire, ignoring all Basil's efforts to calm him. The intruders, now starting on their second jug of wine, were obviously annoyed by the din, for time and again they shouted at the dog in their own language, which only made him more frenzied. Then one of them pulled the pistol from his belt, aimed it at the dog and fired once, then twice, missing each time. We three ducked down from the window, frightened by the gun and its loud bangs. There were more shots, followed by a scream of pain from the dog. The brave warrior fired once again at the tortured animal and the screaming stopped.

After that one of the three men whistled and another soldier entered the yard, took the eggs and departed, followed by the other three. In a few minutes the lorry drew away from the gates. I left the shelter and ran to clasp John's arm for protection.

"It's all right, Lia, these Germans have come to liberate us from the Russian occupation", said my brother. "What a pity they could not have come earlier while Mum was still home!"

Mary looked at the crumpled dog, now lying in a pool of blood. "I hate them, whatever they are doing", she said, stamping her foot. "Why did they have to shoot poor Bob, he couldn't harm them".

"They are not staying in the village, only passing through on their way to fight the Russians", continued John, ignoring Mary, bolstered by his own prowess in being able to speak some German.

Now the lorry had gone, Basil shut the gates. The noise from the heavy machines continued outside from the direction of the main track and the young brother waved to us madly to join him. Crawling along the road were many great grey monster lorries and tanks with huge guns mounted on them, churning up the surface, leaving behind them great gashes in the unmade road and clouds of dust in the air. A few villagers stood by the side of the road waving at the soldiers.

When at last the noise of the vehicles had died away, the squealing of pigs being slaughtered could be heard and a passing neighbour said that there were still some Germans about, taking goods from people. Surely enough when Auntie Alexandra called in she told us that soldiers had stolen and killed her neighbours pig.

"Still, at least they are more civilised than the Russian lot", she said. I thought we were lucky to have got off so lightly with only giving them eggs, cheese and wine.

Once the soldiers had passed through, life in the village returned to some semblance of normality as all the Russian made laws and edicts of the past months were forgotten. People began to smile again and slowly lose their fears. It was little compensation for us having lost our parents and it seemed very cruel for them to have been taken during such a short time of occupation.

A couple of weeks after the German army had passed through a neighbour came to ask us for some salt.

"I don't know what has happened to Isaac. For three days I've been trying the shop, but it's locked and bolted all the time", she said. Then we heard that most of the shops in Bieşti were closed as well and in the past few days no one had seen any of the Jewish shopkeepers from the region. This was a mystery to everyone, for Isaac and the others always opened their shops every day except Saturday. Basil, being inquisitive, checked the store, but surely enough it stayed locked, with the shutters up and a big padlock on the door.

Then one day Constantin came home with an awful story. Three policemen from Kiperceni had gathered together all the Jewish families from the surrounding villages, about seventy people, and told them they were being taken to Orhei for questioning. The group was marched across country for a while until they reached a small ravine. Here the families were ordered to sit and rest. Once all had settled the policemen suddenly opened fire with automatic weapons and killed them. The bodies were pushed into the ravine and covered roughly with earth.

At first I could not believe such a thing, it was too horrible and seemed without reason. Constantin had said the policemen were ordered by the Germans to carry out the act. I heard that the Germans did not like the Jews, but that was no justification for such a terrible thing. John thought perhaps it was just another rumour, for there were many flying about the village. However Isaac and his family did not return.

After the rains came there was a confirmation of what we heard. Going back to college, John and Constantin had to pass the ravine and there they saw uncovered corpses lying in the mud. A few were trapped in the lower branches of trees. The boys were horrified to see this and even more distressed at the sight of abandoned dogs tearing at the bodies. The smell of putrid flesh so sickened them that they hurried away from the scene as fast as they could.

There was a later rumour about Isaac. He and his family had tried to escape from the village when he heard of the intended round up of the Jews, but they were hunted down by the police and killed in a maize field. A hat and shoes belonging to them had been found in this field, but no bodies, so it was assumed someone had buried them. As Marika said, it was all very well talking about the cruel Russians and Germans, but these atrocities had been committed by the local police, although under German orders.

By the time the school holidays ended we were managing fairly well and were quite proud of our achievements especially when one or other of our adult relatives praised us for the way we worked. All six of us were now so united by our sadness and our fears that we felt closer than ever before, but I still missed Mum and Dad so badly that I had many long periods of tears and refused to be comforted. The feeling of safety in their arms, the memories of their patience and gentleness were forever with me. I frequently wondered how they were coping in that Siberian wilderness, and prayed that they would be back soon.

The start of school ordained another change in our lives. There were only Sanda and I left at home, Mary having now to go to attend the college at Orhei, so it was decided that I should stay with Ileana and Sanda with Auntie Alexandra.

With mixed emotions we shut and locked the house, going our different ways. Mary and the boys now had to go to various state boarding schools, being treated as orphans, with free places in their colleges.

With Ileana, I was back in the house where I was born, but how changed everything looked. By now she had a little son, Theodore. Ephraim was away somewhere in the army, leaving Ileana to do all the work on their small farm. At only twenty one, with the boy to look after, she was very happy to have me in the house, for I could take care of Theodore when I was not at school, leaving her free to tend the animals or work in the vegetable plot. The little boy was beginning to walk, so had his hands into everything.

The first winter in the old house was extremely severe with great falls of snow. I struggled to the school in snowdrifts which came up to my knees or more, arriving for classes with frozen hands and sodden boots and socks, which stayed so all day long, to be re-soaked on the way back to Ileana in the afternoon. They all dried out at night on the stove, but were hard and difficult to force on the next day.

The wind howled through the shutters and the thatched roof, while the snow beat with fury against the windows and walls. I was a little frightened at times by the stories of wolves coming into the village to take animals. Ileana had an oil lamp which she kept lit all night in the window, for it was said no wolf would come where a light showed.

My education must have suffered a lot that winter, for during the day at school, with wet cold feet, I could not concentrate enough, and back home Theodore kept me almost fully occupied. All in all the time devoted to homework was very skimpy indeed.

Spring came at last, the snows melted, the meadows were re-carpeted with fresh green, the river tumbled and flowed with renewed vigour, and the storks returned. I stood and looked at the birds whose coming had been such a cheerful event when we were all together in this house.

Memory took me back and I could hear Basil's excited voice calling, "The storks are back, come and see, hurry!" We ran in the yard and watched captivated as the two birds began right away to rebuild the huge nest. Old pieces of twig, branches and unsatisfactory debris were showered indiscriminately on to the thatched roof below as the storks cleaned up. It took them a few days to refurbish the giant nest, about one and a half metres in diameter, with new twigs, small branches, and all the wool, leaves and feathers they needed for the soft cushioning of the expected chicks.

We knew when the eggs had been laid, for one of the birds stayed on the nest almost all the time. One day, however, both of the birds had vacated their base, giving John a naughty idea.

"I'm going to see how many eggs there are", he said with great bravado, "come and help me move the ladder".

"You'll be in trouble if Mum finds out", protested Basil.

"If she finds out we'll know who told her and you'll be in trouble", threatened Constantin, struggling to help John with the ladder. Once it was placed against the roof John shinned up rapidly. He bent over the nest and lifted up one of the large eggs to show us. "There are four this time", he shouted triumphantly. As he returned the egg to its rightful place there was a sudden flash as of a white arrow. One of the birds had gone straight into the attack.

John cried out in pain and fright, clasping one hand to his face, at the same time frantically scrambling down the ladder, almost falling in his haste. Blood was oozing between his fingers.

"I told you not to go!" Basil was all righteousness. "You could have helped with the ladder, you great pudding, then we'd have been quicker. Mary you'd better go tell Mum", ordered Constantin in an aggrieved voice. Mary ran off to return with an anxious mother. Seeing the ladder she guessed at once what had happend.

"You boys, you'll be the death of me. Let me look, John". The stork had gashed his nose. She bathed it with cold water.

"Perhaps that will teach you to leave the poor birds alone. You get on with your games and leave them to their lives".

In two weeks the eggs started to hatch and I could see little heads of wet grey fluff, with permanently open beaks and shut eyes, stretched up on long scraggy necks, awaiting the next meal. Sometimes I spent hours perched on the verandah watching the parent birds in the field beyond the river stepping elegantly on their long red legs looking for some movement that would trigger the pointed red beak to drive into the earth and drag out some unfortunate worm or beetle.

The young birds grew very quickly until they were ready for flight. The parents gave them lessons by pushing them to the very edge of the nest, causing them to flap their wings madly to keep on balance. Then they were allowed to rest. A few lessons and the youngsters chanced their wings and flew to the field. A rest and a clumsy take off brought them back home. In a very short time they joined their parents in the hunt for food.

The storks in flight intrigued me. I thought them as graceful as any ballet dancer, with long necks stretched out in perfect line with their bodies, legs tucked beneath them and large wings beating slowly and evenly, while often, in the thermals, they would glide for long distances with no movement except a slight twist of the wings. They circled and wheeled as leisurely as skaters on an ice-bound lake, to descend finally in smaller and smaller spirals to land neatly on their nests. . .

Now, sadly, here at Ileana's there was only me to look at them.

How much my world had changed from those days filled with warmth, love and happiness! Theodore helped me to forget some of the sadness for my attention was constantly diverted in playing with him, trying to keep him from getting into too many scrapes. Ileana had changed quite a lot, for the disappearance of her family had embittered her and it showed in her face which had once been so full of laughter. I looked forward eagerly for the summer to come to go back to our farm when we had the excitement of opening up the house again to the sun and warmth, and the enjoyment of being together.

By the autumn of 1943 we had spent the third summer in our own house fending for ourselves and felt now very confident with our abilities.

Then, when school started, I went again to Ileana's. In October she had another little boy. I well recall the night she woke me in great agitation. "Wake up, Lia, we must go quickly to our neighbour". I jerked up in bed, still half asleep and slithered down from my perch above the stove, following her blindly, not yet clear headed. She placed a shawl about my shoulders, over my nightie, then took Theodore from his bed and held his hand tightly. By the light of a hurricane lamp, which she carried in the other hand, we followed a path across the orchard to the next house. As we reached the wicker gate Ileana began to shout, desperately.

"Auntie Mary, Auntie Mary!" This aroused the dog which added its furious barking to her shouts. Being awakened by the din, Auntie Mary appeared in the doorway, clad in a white nightgown, looking ghostly in the dim lamplight.

"Sorry to disturb you, Auntie, but I have such violent pains I'm sure it's coming", gasped out Ileana. "In the house, all of you", ordered the older woman in her low hoarse gravelly voice, and led us inside. I was put immediately into a bed with Theodore beside me, and covered with a blanket. "Go back to sleep, Lia, you have school tomorrow". I needed no second bidding. Although curious about Ileana I was much too tired to let it bother me and fell asleep at once.

Next morning I awoke at the crying of a baby. I got out of bed and went into the next room. There Ileana was sitting up, with a baby at her breast.

"Look Lia, the stork has brought Theodore a little brother". I went closer to look at the new arrival, but without great enthusiasm, for by now I had seen several babies that various storks had brought. The mother herself looked pale and exhausted, with dark shadows under her eyes and colourless lips.

"God knows where Ephraim is in the fighting! He will not guess he has another little son now!" Tears gathered in her eyes as she spoke. Auntie Mary, who was sitting by the bed, tried to sound a more cheerful note.

"Don't cry Ileana, when a baby is born it is a happy time, not a sad one. Ephraim must be due for another leave soon, I'm sure, then he'll come home and you'll see how happy he will be".

When I returned from school, Ileana was already back home, with Auntie Mary doing the cooking, in order to give the mother a little more time to rest. As for me, whenever I was not at school I would now have two charges, one to rock in his cradle and the other to play with and keep out of mischief.

FOUR

I was running along one of the small alleyways that divided some of the houses, holding Sanda's hand, urging her to go faster. We had to pass a yard where a big black dog always barked ferociously at me. It was scary to get by him, but we had no choice. We raced past the snarling beast, who leaped madly at the fence. To my utter horror, as we ran by, he broke through and chased after us. In moments I could feel his teeth biting into my shoulder, shaking me.

I opened my eyes, awaking from the awful nightmare, with a rush of relief that there was no dog, but I was still being shaken. Ileana stood over me, her fingers digging into my shoulder.

"Wake up, Lia, you must wake up!" The low insistence of her voice brought back some of the fear of the dream. Something was not right. Except for the once when she was having the baby, Ileana never before had woken me in the night.

"What's the matter?" I asked, confused.

"Get up, Lia, get dressed. John, Basil and Sanda are here, you have to go away with them!" So saying she left the room. Now fully awake I saw Sanda standing at the foot of the bed, silent, white faced, dressed in her grey homespun coat, a red beret on her head, woollen scarf about her neck. I was still bewildered, but had a fleeting moment of pleasure to see that my nice clothes had been laid out on the bed. I dressed quickly in my blue velvet dress with the little flowers, my warm grey wool coat and my white beret. As I slipped on my almost new shoes, still not understanding what was happening, I asked Sanda.

"What are you doing here? Where are we going?"

"I don't know, they came and took me from Auntie Alexandra's", she whispered, on the edge of tears.

Once dressed, I went into the kitchen with Sanda following on my heels. I had been vaguely frightened by the note of urgency in Ileana's voice, alien to her normally calm manner. My fears were not allayed on entering the kitchen, lit brightly with two oil lamps. John was there, together with Basil, talking in low tones to Ileana. The baby was asleep in his cot in the corner. Little Theodore must have been in the other room. Our three elders were obviously worried, their faces strained and pale in the yellow light from the lamps. John turned and spoke to us.

"We have to leave the village now, we must go quickly before anyone sees us!" He was abrupt, commanding.

"Why, John? Why do we have to leave? Where are we going? It's nice here with Ileana!" John was in no mood to explain.

"We just have to, that's all, I'll tell you later. Be good girls and don't argue or cry. We have to hurry!"

My older brother picked up a new leather suitcase and Basil a small wooden one. Ileana handed me a bundle wrapped in a knotted scarf.

"These are your things, keep them with you". I clutched at the proffered belongings, perplexed by the suddeness of events, still not being able to grasp what was happening, where we were going or why. I dared not ask John. I had never seen him before like this, like an adult, serious, no longer the joking extrovert I knew.

Ileana interrupted my thoughts, speaking half to herself.

"Where are you going, you poor things, no money and no parents, to some strange world? You will starve, poor dears!" Her voice was so low and full of anguish I wanted to cry, but John would have been angry. She hugged and kissed us all in turn, then said.

"Go now if you must, God preserve and keep you!"

All five of us went outside into the night, Ileana carrying one of the lamps to light our way. It was not too cold, for by now, in March, the severe bitter weather had given way to the onset of spring. An owl hooted mournfully in the distance, sending a shiver up my spine, for this sound was surely a bad omen. I became aware of a different, nearer noise, of the snuffling movement of cattle. I looked hard in that direction and made out the shape of one of the heavy farm carts. We paused for a moment to accustom our eyes to the darkness, then John led the way to the wagon. Beside the pair of oxen in the shafts stood the short thickset figure of Toma Beiu. He exchanged a few words with John, who turned and lifted us up, one after the other into the cart, floored with a thick layer of straw, rugs spread over.

"Get under the covers and try to sleep. It will be a long way". Basil climbed up without help and tucked in beside Sanda, leaving the other two to mount the driving seat. With a grunted command and a touch of Toma's whip the oxen moved off, towing our carriage. As the iron tyres crunched over the stony ground I looked back and saw Ileana, in the light of the lamp, waving until she became lost in the gloom.

The cart rolled through the silent village until it reached the open road. I wanted to stay awake to see where we were going, but it was not long before I succumbed to the warmth of the straw and rugs, helped by the rocking of the wagon on the uneven surface. My last recollection before I drifted into sleep was of John making the sign of the cross and Basil following suit, murmuring, "God help us". I made the same gesture, without thinking too much about God.

When I awoke it was dawn, the bright glow on the horizon beginning to stain the distant clouds yellow and pink, although overhead the sky was still dark.

"Sanda, look, there are some houses over there!" I pointed my finger.

"That's Orhei, where Mary and I are at college", stated Basil. I had never been this far before, and my curiosity to see the new sights dulled the fears of the past night.

Barely at the outskirts of the town Toma stopped the wagon. John descended, bidding us to do the same, taking our baggage with us. Toma shook John by the hand, gave a little wave to us and, with gutteral cries and frequent use of the whip, turned the animals, lumbering away in the direction from which we had just come.

We were left on some rough grass beside an old house built of clay bricks. John looked at us and said.

"The three of you stay here while I go into the town. I don't know how long I'll be!" He placed his leather case carefully on top of Basil's wooden box and strode off quickly. In the fawn military style raincoat he looked now every inch a man. With my bewildered head full of so many sights and sounds I watched him walk towards the silhouetted buildings.

Once John was out of earshot I pestered Basil with all the questions I had not dared to ask before.

"Why have we left the village, Basil? Where are we going? Where has John gone? Where are Constantin and Mary?"

"Wait a minute", he said patiently, "I'll tell you all I know about it. We have to leave the village because the Russians are coming back again to occupy this region, so we have to go to some other part of the country where they will not come".

"But why can't we stay even if they are coming back?"

"Because they would not let us live in Slobozia, they would send us away, like Mum and Dad, to that horrible Siberia".

"I don't want to go to Siberia, I want to go home", interrupted Sanda tearfully.

"I know, but we can't. Anyway, John has gone to find about buses or something to get us to Kishnev and from there a train will take us to Iaşi. As for Mary, you know she was staying with the Mitrofans. Well, they have taken her with them to Bucharest. Constantin will meet us in Kishnev".

It was chilly waiting in the early morning, without the rugs and the warmth of the two cuddled bodies beside me. Basil pulled his dark overcoat more tightly about him. I was beginning to feel hungry and regretted not asking for something to eat while we were still with Ileana. Some time passed before John returned. His face was set and taut, having had no success.

"There is no chance of a bus. We shall just have to walk, there's no other way".

We all picked up our belongings and headed into Orhei. There were people about now, more and more coming on to the road as we walked further into the town. They came from every side and all were hurrying. Most had bundles or cases of some sort. The road soon filled with carts, some pulled by cattle, others by horses. A few of the horses were being ridden, with bags and packages lashed about the animals neck and belly. Whole families were struggling with handcarts piled high with household goods. There were many bicycles being pushed, laden with great weights of belongings.

The street was now paved with flat shiny stones, on which the wheels of the carts clattered and rang as they jerked from one cobble to another. How confusing it was, but new and exciting as well! The houses were so tall, some being two floors, some even three, nearly all built of stone or brick. The roofs were of tiles or green metal sheets, not thatch or wooden shingles. Compared with the village houses they looked so imposing and so large and solid.

Here even the people had a different air about them. Apart from the haste, which was certainly not the pace of life in our village, they were dressed in brighter, smarter clothes, wearing coats of better materials, some of fur, with hats of unusual shapes. Many of the women sported thin shoes with high heels, their legs clad in silk stockings. They had made up faces, with red cheeks and lips, ears and necks adorned with jewellery. I looked with some envy at the better clothes of the children, girls with patent leather shoes and bows of coloured ribbon in their hair. Although I wore my best clothes I felt and looked very much out of place in this town.

Many of the houses were obviously abandoned, I thought, with doors and windows hanging open. Curtains streamed from some of the openings, flapping lazily in the slight breeze. Window panes had broken, with pieces of curtain clinging to the jagged teeth. All sorts of goods and trinkets were strewn across the path: dozens of cards, toys and broken ornaments. Some looked so pretty I wanted to pick them up, but John would have none of it.

"There's no time for that, just leave them, we have a long way to go."

There were many dogs, all pitifully thin, with ribs showing, heads and tails drooping dejectedly, sniffing and scraping at anything which might be food. They looked at us mournfully as we passed, having given up expecting anything but kicks and shouts from the humans.

The throng of vehicles and people, all moving purposefully in the same direction, began to swell with even more traffic. Motor lorries in khaki colours, full of German soldiers, now added to the press. They hooted and roared pushing their way through the slower traffic, most of which moved out of the way to let them pass. My pace slowed often in my wonder and amazement to see all these unfamiliar things, my head turning from side to side so as not to miss any part of this spectacle. John had constantly to push Sanda and me to go faster, urging us with the necessity of moving, hurrying.

I saw, gathered at the entrances to houses, many groups saying their farewells, some weeping profusely, kissing and hugging, shaking hands. So many times was I to hear: "God help us, what will happen? When shall we ever see you again?"

With many pauses and stops and much persuading from John, the four of us reached the other side of the town. Here the cobbles gave way once more to a dirt track. The pavement ended, forcing us into the stream of vehicles. It became much more difficult to keep up the pace as we were being constantly buffetted from one side then the other, lorries and carts forcing their way through the human flood. Huge trees lined the road, confining all to the width of the track, preventing the crowds from spreading into the fields at either side.

Many more soldiers in lorries, some with red crosses emblazoned on the sides, some with smaller jeep like trucks, joined in the melee, all straining to get away from the Russian threat. Sanda and I were tired, my feet hurt and hunger tortured me. Both of us began to whine and sob a little.

In despair John adopted the tactic of pulling us into the path of any lorry, waving at it to stop and give us lifts. Time and again he tried and time and again he failed as the trucks, ignoring his pleas, forced us out of their paths. Sanda began to cry with the pain of blistered feet.

Unexpectedly, at another despairing try, one of the lorries stopped. John spoke to the driver in halting German, pointing insistently at us girls, now in floods of tears.

"Stop crying and get into this lorry quickly. The soldiers will take you with them". We both looked at the three men in the cab and shrank back against our brother. In their grey uniforms, with guns sticking up between them, they looked just like the Germans who had shot our dog. Sensing us hesitate, John shouted angrily. "Do as I say, no one will hurt you. Get up in the cab or you will have to walk all the way!" Behind the lorry the column of vehicles had been forced to halt. There were hoots and shouts as they became impatient with the delay. John picked me up bodily and thrust me into the arms of the nearest soldier, who dragged me inside. Basil pushed Sanda up behind me.

"These men will take you to Kishnev. Wherever they put you down, and however long it is you must stay there until we find you, otherwise you will be lost!"

The lorry restarted its journey, leaving John and Basil at the roadside. I miserably watched them be swallowed up in the crowd. Two of the Germans had lifted us up onto their knees and smiled at us. They were all at once less frightening. The one on whose lap I was sitting touched my hair occasionally. A few times he patted his chest and said "Hans", but I did not understand that he was trying to ask my name, so remained silent. The other soldier fished in his pocket and gave each of us a few sweets, while the driver concentrated on getting through the throng.

Once I realised there was nothing to fear from these men my interest in the passing world was rekindled. By now the crowd had begun to thin out and the driver could make much better progress, the slow carts keeping to one side to let the motor vehicles pass. I was amazed there were so many communities and such great numbers of people. I was sleepy but determined to stay awake. Sanda, however, began to nod and in a few minutes was sleeping in the arms of the man holding her. The soldiers were talking amongst themselves and although I could not understand a word, the strain showed on their faces. It was easy for me now to recognise these expressions of worry.

Buildings on the outskirts of a town started to appear, the road becoming once again cobbled. The driver flashed a glance at us. "Kishnev", he stated. This was where John said we would be taken. The lorry stopped by a piece of waste land, the driver descended, walked around the vehicle and helped us down from his compatriots. Then he remounted and drove away. The other two Germans looked at us with pity, said something in their language, which I suppose was a farewell, and waved to us as the truck pulled again into the traffic stream.

We stood for a while at the edge of the road, looking towards the direction from which our brothers would come, clutching our bundles. We walked away from the road on to the piece of land covered with thick weeds and grass. Tired and hungry we sat down, watching the stream of people and vehicles roll by in an unending flood. I wondered where all these people, carts, lorries and horses could come from. Sanda fell asleep against me, but I had to stay awake, for she was now my responsibility. I had no idea how long we should have to wait. How long would it take John and Basil to walk. If they came by night how could they possibly find us? This whole new world was so overwhelming. Such different buildings, so many hurrying frightened people. There was a tension, a feeling of fear all about me. I felt so alone and abandoned with all this great crowd rushing past ignoring Sanda and me. What could I do if John and Basil did not arrive? I was so frightened I began to cry, which woke Sanda.

"Why are you crying?"

"I need to go to the toilet", I lied, trying to conceal my fears from her.

"Well, go over there by the weeds, and I'll stand in front so no one can see!"

The never ending flow of traffic lost its definition and became a many hued blanket of ever changing shape undulating past, the noise of wheels and hooves blended into a general murmur of sound as of an approaching storm which never materialised. We waited on the patch of grass for such a long time, many hours I suppose. I was hungry and thirsty and getting more miserable by the minute and very afraid, when, to my great relief, I saw my two dear brothers come running from the crowd. We rushed to them and held on to them as though they had been away for months.

"We must go quickly to the station and catch a train", said John. Such exciting news helped me trot along more eagerly, my hunger temporarily forgotten. I had never seen any trains, but had heard about them. I really wanted to see one of these wonders which were so difficult for me to imagine.

The whole world of faces moved with us in the same direction, all dusty grim and tired. Many children were walking with parents or relatives, all looking unhappy and miserable.

Passing a low embankment a whistle shrieked somewhere behind us. Basil exclaimed. "Hear that? It's a train whistle!" Minutes after a monster black engine came into view, puffing out thick clouds of smoke and steam, crawling slowly, towing a line of tankers. I was quite perplexed. How did people get into these things? Where were the doors and windows I had heard about? I did not want to sound silly so did not ask the questions in my mind. No one had ever explained that trains did anything else but carry people. Shortly after, however, all was revealed to my puzzled brain, when another engine snorted by, towing real carriages. I was so relieved that we did not have to get into the big round tanks!

The station was jammed with a great mass of people and baggage. They spread out into the forecourt like a thick coarse coloured carpet of humanity. Some were in agitated groups, standing and gesticulating, some wandering about the fringes, seemingly uncertain of where to go or what to do, but most were sitting or lying down resignedly amongst bags, cases and bundles. There was no way across without walking over and amongst the churning mass of bodies, certainly no place to sit. John led us through this grey faced worn looking crowd, until we came to one of the iron pillars supporting the roof of the station.

"Stay here", he said, "I've got to find Constantin". He edged into the crowd slowly, doing his best to avoid stepping on too many legs. I asked the ever helpful Basil. "Is Constantin here in the station?" My brother was leaning against the metal column, his eyes drooping, shoulders sagging with fatigue, but he answered me gently. I was surprised at times that he did not get angry or lose his temper, like Constantin, with my eternal questions, but temper had never been part of his nature.

"Constantin came with John to the station two days ago to see if the trains were running, then he remained to get tickets for us. There were so many people no one knew how long they would have to wait".

"But why is it all such a rush now? No one said we'd have to go away until today?"

"Because John and Constantin, being here in the college, heard about the Russians coming soon. There may be little time left before they close the border, then no one will be able to get out!"

I could not put this Russian threat into perspective, but seeing all the desperate people around made me aware that some terrible thing was frightening them, and I felt frightened as well, without knowing exactly why.

"Did John come all the way from here to Slobozia just for us?"

"Yes, and he called for me at Orhei. He had to walk and get lifts like we did today". Poor John, I thought, he must be exhausted.

He returned about half an hour later with Constantin, who also looked very tired, for he had queued up all night to get the tickets. Meanwhile John had managed to buy some bread and cheese for us, which we devoured rapidly and greedily, appeasing our hunger for the time being.

A train was due in an hour. We were told to go to the toilets in preparation for the journey. These were also full of people, filthy, and stank to high heaven. On the way back we waited our turn at the water fountain and were cursed several times as we tripped and stepped on a few of the resting bodies. Together again, following John, we picked up our belongings and eased through the jam towards the platform. By the time a whistle in the distance announced the arrival of the train we were in a better position to fight our way aboard.

The sound from the engine aroused the mass of people, who rose as one, grabbing cases and bags and pushing towards the line. We held grimly on to the boys and our bundles, forcing ourselves to stay upright. Everyone was fighting to get to the steps of the already overcrowded coaches.

We could make no progress at all in the crowd milling about the entrances. The boys suddenly pulled us away from the crush, dragging us further along the carriage. Looking up at the windows I could see another mass of faces, but John had an idea. At one of the open windows he, with Constantin's help, heaved me up towards the opening. "Climb in, Lia", they shouted.

A voice from above was screaming, "No room, no room!" but we ignored it. I scrabbled at the window and fell in awkwardly on the nearest passengers. Sanda was bundled in in the same way before anyone could protest further, our two bundles being flung in after us.

"We will find you later", shouted John. By the time we had scrambled to our feet, breathless and bruised, the brothers were nowhere to be seen. It was almost impossible to find space to stand, so tightly crowded was the corridor with travellers. As we struggled to stay upright, the door to the nearest compartment opened and a woman said. "Put those two little girls in here". I held tightly to my bundle as someone picked me up and dumped me bodily into the compartment, closely followed by Sanda. I tried to settle myself on the cases filling most of the floor space.

The train rumbled off and my worries returned, for I could not believe that our brothers had boarded the train, and we were left amongst these strange people.

The woman who had been instrumental in getting us into the compartment asked our names and wanted to know if our parents were with us. When I explained shyly that Mum and Dad had been taken to Siberia, and we were running away from our village together with our brothers, she started to curse venemously everything Russian, with intense hatred for such a cruel and stupid system. The rest of the occupants joined in the general condemnation. Another woman pulled a round loaf from her bag, broke off some pieces which she gave to her three children, handing what was left to Sanda and me, saying. "You poor dears must be famished". There were three men and four women as well as the three other children squashed into the small space. Some bags were on the floor between the seats, all the racks above being tightly packed with other luggage. The atmosphere was awful, with two men smoking as well. How I longed to be back in the fresh clean air of my village and not in this dreadful overpacked train, banging and rattling on its slow journey. Despite all, the rocking of the coach and fatigue had its effect and I found myself dropping off to sleep. Sanda was lolling against me already. I was quite proud of her, for she had not cried much during all this strange ordeal, seeming just to accept what came to pass.

When I awoke the train was at a standstill. One of the men shouted through the open window "How long are we staying here?" and turned to us with the reply.

"We are on a siding to let some military trains pass, we could be here for hours. I'm going out to stretch my legs". He worked his way into the corridor with some difficulty. Most of the passengers in the passageway had taken the opportunity to get out of the coach, but desperate as I was to go to the toilet I was afraid to leave the little haven. Then, to my delight, I heard John outside shouting, "Lia, Lia, where are you?" I wriggled to the window and returned his shout.

"We are here!"

"Come down, the train will stay here a long time. I have some food for you". With Sanda following, I clambered through the jumble of packages, bags and people and descended from the coach. All three brothers were waiting at the coach steps.

"How did you get on the train?" I asked.

"They attached some flat wagons at the end, we're on one of those", said Basil, pointing to the rear of the chain of coaches.

We ate the food that John gave us, just more bread and cheese, and drank water from a bottle, then my brother said. "You had better return to your places. The journey will take a long time as we are going another way, but whenever the train stops like now we'll come to see you".

In the compartment the cases and bags had been rearranged, giving us a little more room. We could both now sit on something softer.

Coming later to his seat, one of the men said breathlessly "The bridge to Iaşi has been destroyed, we've got to go via Galatsi". There was a groan of despair from the women at such bad news.

"How long will that take, it's a hell of a distance?"

"I know, but it's the only bridge left over the Prut. It may take days because all the military trains get priority".

Our train stayed put for hours while others, I suppose the military ones the man had mentioned, rumbled past. We finally moved, travelling slowly for several hours until the train stopped once more in a siding near a station.

Here the local peasants came with baskets of food for sale, and as once again most of the passengers left the coaches, I looked out for the brothers. I was happy to see John by the track bargaining with one of the food sellers, an elderly woman, and soon after he beckoned us down, giving us some bread and the bottle, now filled with milk. When we had finished eating he saw us climb back into the carriage and returned to whatever place he had found for himself.

It took three days in all to reach Galatsi, days of slow, cramped and weary travel that must have exhausted all on the train. John had been as good as his word, buying food from the peasants who gathered at most of the stops. There was not much variety, but we did not go very hungry.

I was dozing away on the third day when suddenly one of the women shouted.

"The Prut, the Prut, thank God at last". She crossed herself two or three times. I looked out at this river which seemed to mean so much. Between its banks water from the melting mountain snows rushed in foaming torrents. The noise of the wheels changed from a flat clackety clack to a hollow booming sound as the train began to cross the metal bridge which marked the border into the part of Romania where we should all be safe. The speed then increased and the stops became less frequent. At each station passengers now descended and very few boarded. Before very long my brothers were able to climb into our coach, and Sanda and I joined them in the corridor.

"Now, girls", said John, "We are going to Sighişoara!"

"To Sighişoara? Why there? This train is going to Bucharest, surely we'd be better off in the capital?" Constantin demanded angrily.

"I don't think so, I'm afraid that Bucharest will be bombed to hold up the German retreat, whereas there's nothing to be bombed in Sighişoara. Anyhow I heard that the Bessarabian refugees are being dealt with there".

"I still think we should go to Bucharest" insisted Constantin, doggedly.

"Will you take the chance and risk our lives if the place gets bombed?" asked John. Basil, not wanting to upset Constantin, said in a small voice. "I'm scared of being bombed and would rather go to Sighişoara".

"I wish we hadn't come on this rotten train, I don't want to be bombed either", cried Sanda, having no more idea than me what bombing was. I stayed silent, not knowing which of my brothers was right.

"Very well, John, you always think you know best, we'll go to Sighişoara", reluctantly agreed Constantin.

The three boys all looked very tired, faces and hands dirty with the grit and smoke collected while sitting on the open wagon. John, although grimy, had somehow managed to keep his raincoat quite clean. They all sat on their cases and tried to sleep until we had to change trains at Ploeşti, where we descended into another seething mass of people. Again it was a fight to get aboard the train to Braşov, where we would also have to change, but with five sets of feet and elbows working overtime we forced our way into a coach. This journey, sitting in the corridor, lasted a mere three hours.

By the time we arrived at Braşov I was utterly worn out and thankful to step on to solid ground.

"We are all so tired, I think it best to stay here for a day or so before going on to Sighişoara. What do you think?" asked John. We all agreed immediately. The conditions on the train had been bad enough for me, but for my poor brothers it must have been horrendous to spend three days outside on the flat truck.

We went to the washroom, for John refused to search for a place to stay until the three of them looked more presentable. We then found a small hotel in a side street. I thought it was the height of luxury, from the bouncy white beds to the flushing porcelain toilet, which was incredible. Water came from taps in the room, not from a well, and one even had hot water. All these new things intrigued me greatly. We stayed two days and then it was time to make another train journey to the final destination.

At our arrival in Sighişoara we found a reception centre set up in the station, dealing with refugees.

"Hello, do you want help?" asked a woman in Red Cross uniform.

"Yes, replied John, "These are my brothers and sisters, we are from Bessarabia. Our parents were deported to Siberia and we have no money and nowhere to go!"

"There are many children like you", replied the woman kindly, "but there's no need to worry. Wait here a few minutes". She returned shortly, and said to John. "First of all you have to fill in these forms. For the time being your sisters must go to a reception centre in town, and you three brothers to Seleuş, not far from here.

John dealt with the forms she needed, then the brothers joined a group of boys who were waiting nearby while Sanda and I were left in charge of another official who was organising the girls. The two refugee centres were not far apart and we hoped to see each other before long.

When our group had grown to about twenty girls, one of the Red Cross workers gave us packets of food. Everyone immediately opened them and sat down on bags and cases to eat. It was funny, I thought, to have a kind of picnic in a railway station.

After the food had vanished we were formed into a double column, with the youngest, who happened to be Sanda and me, in front. Older girls, students from the university, came at the rear. We marched through the streets until we halted at a large three floored building painted yellow, set back from the road. This was our destination. We entered a wide cobbled yard where a lady speaker welcomed us to the town and told us that we would stay in the building for a while. Inside we found a freshly painted dormitory full of beds covered in brown blankets. Sanda and I claimed adjoining beds and sorted out our small bundles into a nearby cupboard. I eagerly awaited the bell which was to be rung for mealtimes. When it sounded everyone hurried to the dining hall where I had the first hot meal since leaving the village. John's money, from selling some goods from the house, was very limited, and he had not been able to afford both the hotel room and meals. We had survived on very basic rations. But now we had soup, roast lamb and a dessert called 'Bird's Milk'.

I like this better then cow's milk", said Sanda, tasting it with curiosity. I was puzzled by the name. How could they milk birds? This bothered me until one enlightened girl explained that it was made with eggs and milk, so it was *birds* from eggs and *milk* from cows. There seemed such an awful lot I did not know.

The first few days passed with the routine of getting rid of lice. We were bathed each day, hair washed and combed with thick combs to drag out the insects. Our clothing was treated with paraffin, and some badly affected girls had to have their hair shaved off. All had picked up infestations while travelling in crowded trains, crushed together with people who had had no means of washing perhaps for weeks. Several days of treatment freed us from the pests.

There was little to do at that centre except eat, sleep and play. Older girls had to help in the kitchen or with other domestic tasks, and some of them tried to teach us different games or songs.

One day a loud wailing sound sent us rushing into the yard. We were screamed at by some of the staff to run away from the town because enemy aeroplanes were coming. Sanda and I followed the senior girls, fleeing as fast as we could from the building and up a sloping hill towards some woods. Hundreds of people were swarming up like a crowd of ants. Shortly after the shelter of the woods was reached the droning sound of warplanes filled the air.

"They must be going to Ploeşti, where the oilfields are, I think", said someone. Whoever spoke was probably right, as the aircraft passed overhead and flew away into the distance. Getting happily to my feet I could now look down on Sighişoara.

From this vantage point a great panorama opened to the West where the town entrance was marked by a small tower. To the East forest covered hills sloped down gently to a large meadow. The town itself looked picturesque with a castle perched high in a cluster of medieval houses painted in bright colours: blues, pinks, yellows and greens. A river threaded its lazy way past the foot of the hill. Suddenly the clock in the castle tower struck the hour and my attention was caught by the sight of little brightly painted wooden human figures set below the clock starting to move round the tower in circles, banging miniature drums. I was absolutely fascinated because I had never seen a clock like this before. From then on I looked anxiously for the hour to strike and the little figures to perform their dance for me.

I stayed for a while on the hill, looking at the tranquil scene, with the warm sun, set in an azure sky, playing gently on my back. One of the older girls, Veronica, asked me if I could draw the shape of Romania. With a stick I drew the outline on a patch of earth, the older girl holding my arm and correcting my mistakes. When my poor drawing was completed, she took the stick from me and hatched across the regions of Bessarabia and Bucovina.

"See, Lia, in a few days these rich regions of our country where you and I were born will not belong to Romania any more. They will be occupied by the Russians who will impose their communist way of life there", she said bitterly.

Being so young I could not understand completely what she meant but I did know that we should never be able to return home because of this occupation. I was saddened by the thought and wondered miserably how my parents would be able to find us if they ever returned from Siberia. Tears came to my eyes. It had already been so long since I had seen them, since I had known their love and comfort. Perhaps I should never see them again. I tried not to think about that, it was just too awful.

At that moment Sanda came and took my hand. We wandered for a little while in the woods, talking about the aeroplanes which we had seen and the bombs which we had not. Next day I heard that Ploeşti and Bucharest had been bombed, with many buildings destroyed and set on fire and many people killed.

A few days after the attack on Bucharest I was astounded to see Mary amongst a group of newcomers. With great joy we hugged and embraced each other. She looked quite grown up in a pretty flowered dress and white sandals.

"How did you get here?" I asked, "I haven't seen you since Christmas".

"John and Constantin brought me".

"Where from, Bucharest?"

"No, I was in Mileşti, near Craiova. You know I went with the priest's family, the Mitrofan's, to Bucharest?"

"Yes, I thought you were still there?"

"The priest was afraid that Bucharest would be bombed, so he took us all to a sister he has in Mileşti. Then unexpectedly John and Constantin turned up and brought me back with them so we could all be together".

Years later I heard the full horrific story.

After the very severe raid on Bucharest the two brothers decided to go there, find Mary and bring her to Sighişoara where she would be safer. On the sixth of April they set out. It was difficult to get into the capital for the trains were chaotic and crowded, with long delays, but eventually they reached the city. There everything was in a turmoil, for much of the town had been destroyed. No buses or trams were running, the streets being blocked with rubble.

After a long walk they found the given address, only to see, to their great consternation, that the house was completely wrecked. They made enquiries and heard that some of the victims had been taken to the medical school. Once there both were shocked beyond measure to see some hundreds of corpses laid out in the courtyard, covered only with sheets of newspaper. Many of them were so badly mutilated, with limbs and even heads torn off that John and Constantin had to give up looking for Mary, it was much too grim for them to continue.

Then, luckily, Constantin remembered the address of a family related to the priest, and going there, they found out, with great relief, that the Mitrofans and Mary had gone to Mileşti.

By now, exhausted with the journey and the trauma of their search, the two brothers booked into a hotel with the idea of setting out afresh the next day. It was not to be, for in the night the syrens screamed out, heralding another raid. The boys awoke in panic, dressed and fled to the railway station, hoping for a train to get them out of the city and to Craiova to search for Mary.

When the train did arrive it was packed, but determined not to be left to face any bombing they climbed on to the steps of one of the coaches, clinging to the handrails. Constantin was so tired that he dozed off. John saw this and had to hold both himself and his brother on to their precarious perch.

At the next stop someone had opened the window of a toilet compartment and John helped Constantin climb in through the narrow opening, while he himself, unable to follow unaided, stayed on the step.

At Craiova John descended, but could not find Constantin on the crowded platform. All the older brother could do was wait in the station, hoping that sooner or later Constantin would show up. After a few hours, during which time John slept on a seat, Constantin arrived. He had fallen asleep on the floor of the coach and had not woken until the train terminated at Turnu Severin, from where he had to return to Craiova.

Together again they went to the Mileşti address, where Mary was staying and took her with them for the return journey to Sighişoara. She had a fairly heavy suitcase containing all she had from college, which the brothers carried to the station with the aid of a stick pushed through the handle. While waiting for the train in Craiova station another air raid warning sounded. Scared stiff they ran into a field, leaving the case on the platform.

Hearing the 'All Clear' they returned to the station to find, to their amazement, the suitcase still there. They were sure it would have been stolen. The rest of the journey was without incident.

In the refugee centre, Mary, now nearly fourteen, was put in a different group from us, but we saw her frequently. Sighişoara was merely a temporary stop and soon we were to be transferred to somewhere else. Where would we be going now and what would it be like? My world had been turned upside down so many times in such a short period.

FIVE

We had been given some rough cloth haversacks which we now packed and were very soon ready to depart. Outside on the road a line of carts was drawn up, each pulled by two huge black oxen with long curled horns, so very unlike our brown and white cattle at home. These beasts looked to me so ugly and threatening with their great horns and black bodies. We piled our bags onto the carts and the oxen lumbered on their way. Younger girls were allowed to ride but all others had to walk alongside.

The variety of cases and bags, from new leather suitcases to wooden boxes and our rough cloth sacks, gave a good indication of the cross section of class and wealth from which the refugee children had come. I thought about the abandoned homes which I had seen in Orhei, and speculated as to whether any of these girls were from there.

Once out of the pretty town of Sighişoara, we bumped, rolled and jerked in the creaking clumsy carts at the low pace set by the oxen. Each wagon had a driver sitting on a plank seat at the front, who constantly urged on the animals with a strange gutteral sound. He also had a whip made from a long stick with a tassle of leather bound to one end, which he rhythmically flicked at the beasts.

After about three hours journey we reached the village of Daneş, our destination. By now I was hungry, thirsty and covered in a film of grey dust, as was everything on the carts. The village itself looked unusual to me with the houses, lining each side of the road, being joined to each other with high wooden fences, making it impossible to see into any of the yards. Each house had an equally high wooden gate to keep visitors out or cattle in. When we reached the far end of the village the carts stopped in front of the largest building. It was two floors high, painted yellow and protected by a grassy bank, on which grew several conifers. A tall wooden fence enclosed the building and its grounds. Above the main door a sign stated 'Daneş Refugee Camp'. A few villagers looked at us curiously and we at them, each wondering about the other. We picked up our baggage and entered the premises to be welcomed by a small group of ladies who were to take care of us. They showed us our quarters in the building, a primary school which had been converted into dormitories and a dining room.

After leaving our luggage we were taken into the courtyard to wash at some stone troughs placed near a well; there being no running water in this village. Soap and towels were laid on a wooden board for our use. The toilets were a far cry from the relative modernity of Sighişoara. Under a sheltering corrugated roof long wooden boards at seat height, with holes cut at intervals, covered a cesspit. There were no divisions between the holes, no privacy at all. Fortunately soon after our arrival some enterprising girls made partitions between each toilet seat with pieces of cloth hung from poles.

Everywhere in the camp was clean and neat, with pots and jars of wild flowers as decoration. The first round of exploration was cut short by the ringing of a bell. A different bell, but the same message, food! Long tables and benches, as in Sighişoara, filled the dining room and the food was good and very welcome. The cook, a rather beefy lady in a white coat, smiled at us indulgently as we tucked into the meal she had prepared.

After the lunch I sat, with other girls, on the grassy bank at the front of the building and looked down on the village. No one passed to make it more interesting.

Within the next few days a lady doctor came to examine us. Sanda and I were pronounced much too thin and underweight and were listed to have extra food. However, we would not eat some of the dishes, which were strange to us. This did not upset the cook, as I expected, but on the contrary she kindly tried to prepare for us only the meals we preferred.

The camp had a clothes store run by a jolly little lady. I liked her right away for her cheerful smile and I think she liked me, for one day she invited Sanda and me into her store and gave us various clothes to try on. She must have known we had very little, for she outfitted us with dresses, nighties, shoes and underwear. I thought myself very rich in this new place.

There was, however, quite a stern discipline, although administered with a great deal of kindness and understanding. At the first sound of the bell in the morning we had to rush from bed into the yard and, in our pyjamas, do ten minutes of gymnastics to wake us up, run back, wash, dress and make our beds, which had to be properly done as they were sometimes checked for hollows and bumps with a level stick. Then breakfast, which was the best part, followed by the morning parade and the announcement of our day's programme, which varied from day to day to prevent us becoming bored.

We had been divided into seven groups, each of which had one day's work duty; cleaning the camp, including the toilets, preparing the vegetables for meals, setting and clearing the tables and washing the dishes. The ethic to work was instilled into us, as well as the need to do everything in a neat and tidy fashion. Competition with other groups stimulated the girls to do things, such as arranging the flowers or decorating the tables, in different or better ways.

Most of the time the programme for the day was thought out by the group itself, with treasure hunts in the woods, games, or new songs to learn.

Once a week each group had a clothes washday, when a great deal of hard work had to be done, for the water had to be brought from the well, fires lit under the huge coppers, which then needed a constant supply of wood and water fed to them. Then, of course, came the actual washing of the clothes with basic soap and crude rubbing boards. While the hot water was available the girls also managed to have showers, using either a large watering can with a fine rose, pouring the water over each other, or a large tin with holes punched in the bottom, tied to a post. It was a busy work day, but with some fun and lots of water to splash and play with.

The kitchen garden behind the school was also tended by us. Weeding, hoeing, planting and harvesting all fell to our lot, for there were only five staff to keep the camp running; the headmistress, the administrator, the cook and her helper and the stores lady.

The girls who knew how to sew were often sitting under the shade of the trees, making petticoats from white cotton material, which the camp issued. The older girls who could use sewing machines spent quite a lot of time making uniforms for us all. These were as simple as possible, a navy blue skirt and a white blouse, with a piece of tricoloured material, the national colours, fashioned into a neckerchief.

Cleaning the nearby church and decorating it was another task set us, and here the older girls had good opportunities to vie with the others in flower arranging.

The days were filled with outdoor activities and sports. There were also little entertainments when each group sang songs, danced or recited poems. Sometimes a huge camp fire was lit in the evenings, and this I loved for it was so enthralling to hear the pine wood crackle and to watch the blazing fire send myriads of sparks fluttering and twinkling up into the night sky. Everyone listened to the older girls tell stories while sitting round the fire.

I adored sports days, with competition between the groups, or between our camp and the refugee boys camp from Seleuş, when we would all try to outdo each other in running, jumping, volleyball or tennis. On such a day I had the added bonus of being able to see my brothers again, to hug them once more.

The life in the camp was wonderful. We were well fed, could play, walk freely about the village and countryside in perfect safety. How exciting to take off shoes and splash through the puddles which followed summer showers, for summer was always beautiful, with blue skies above. Some girls sunbathed on the grass, or read under the shade of the trees.

In this warm atmosphere of the camp so many friendships were made, so many stories were told to each other of happiness, sadness, deprivation and sometimes of horror, so many things which should not have happened to children, some of whom would be marked for life with their terrible experiences.

Several of the older girls played, in many ways, the roles of substitute mothers, by adopting one or more of us youngsters to look after. They washed our hair, checked our clothes and made sure we were generally contented. Of course, unavoidable times of loneliness and sadness occurred when thinking of my parents, wondering where they were, what was happening to them, and most dreadful of all, whether I should see them again. Often a few words would spark off memories of happier years in the past when all our family was together. Some nights I cried in bed, thinking that Mum and Dad could easily be dead in some Siberian wasteland. I felt terribly homesick at times for I missed my parents so much.

We had an enforced hour of rest after lunch, which was another time for thinking, as I could never sleep. I waited anxiously for the bell to sound its song of freedom, when I could go outside once more. There was always so much to see, to delight the eye; the dozens of multicoloured butterflies dancing about the wild flowers, blooming resplendent with their bells and hoods and petal rings, their leaves of many shades of green, some long sword like shapes, some oval, some round and crinkled.

I was still fascinated by the big black oxen which pulled the farm carts piled high with straw or hay, pumpkins, melons or wood. They seemed to look deliberately at me as though to frighten me, and if they did so they succeeded very well. The local chidren, however, had no such fears and often the load of hay was topped by a bevy of small laughing faces poking out from the stack, like chicks in a huge nest. The father walked alongside the beasts, making the usual grrr-grrr noise in his throat, touching them with the long whip.

The cattle lumbered by in a rhythm of tossing heads and swishing tails, vainly attempting to rid themselves of the eternally irritating flies. Although the man's whip and grunts did not disturb them, the sight of anything red did so very much, and I had to be very careful indeed when crossing the fields if any of the black animals were about, to be sure to not have any clothes of the offending colour, for this would send them careering at full tilt across the meadow, heads down, nostrils flared and snorting, and the vicious horns in battle position.

The life in camp was very pleasant until August, when the whole atmosphere changed dramatically. The older girls now spent more and more time gathered in little groups around a radio which the headmistress possessed, listening with strained attention to the news bulletins, whispering to each other and looking worried and anxious, and they had less time for us younger ones. Whenever I tried to find out what was happening they fobbed me off with, "It's nothing, nothing for you to bother your head about, Lia, you just go and play with Sanda.".

However, one day a special assembly was called when the headmistress told us with great sadness that the camp was to be closed.

"I have gathered you here because I have some bad news to tell you. Probably some of you already have heard that the German army is being forced to retreat by the Russians. At the same time our country, under the leadership of the Communist party, has changed sides and joined the Allies. This means that Russian troops will soon be marching through Romania. As everyone fears the behaviour of these Russian soldiers the Refugee Committee has decided, for your protection, to close the camp. You have no need to worry, for you will all go to some villages where the people have already offered, with open arms, to look after you until boarding school starts, and things have settled down once more".

That was such an awful day for all of us. Everyone spoke of nothing but the war and these terrible Russians who would be coming.

Where was I to go now? What sort of family would I be with? Would Sanda and Mary be with me or apart? It had been so peaceful and pleasant in Daneş until now, but the beautiful dream was about to be shattered. The night after the bad news I just could not sleep.

In the next few days we were busy packing, cleaning and storing all the camp equipment. When the time to leave our beautiful camp came I could not stop weeping. I walked to the back of the building to look again at the familiar fields, then I said my tearful goodbyes to the friends I had made, who were going to different places from me. Mary, Sanda and I, together with some other girls, went by horse and cart to a village called Laslea. We stopped outside the Mayor's house where a crowd had gathered, awaiting our arrival, chattering and gesticulating to each other. On our approach all turned to look at us, the conversation dying. We descended with our luggage and stood in a row, waiting.

The mayor, important this day, told us that the gathered people were there to take us to their homes. He made the most of his day of glory, his red face glowing with the effort of his speech. For the occasion he had donned a suit, which elevated his importance above that of the traditionally dressed peasants.

"We welcome you dear girls to our little village and hope you will be happy with us. All these good people are here to look after you, I now leave them to come forward and take you to their homes!"

The older and stronger girls, Mary amongst them, were chosen quickly, while the younger ones, including Sanda and me, were left waiting. Seeing us standing there, the student who was in charge of us said.

"Sisters cannot be separated, so whoever takes the oldest one must also take the youngest". As a result Mary was promptly returned to the group, but not for long because the local priest kindly offered to have her and Sanda. I was very crestfallen now to be left without them and felt no happier when a man with a thick drooping moustache and dirty working clothes came with his wife to choose me. She asked, in quite a pleasant voice, whether I would like to stay with them. Although I did not care for the appearance of the man I feared the consequences of refusing, so answered "Yes" in a low subdued voice. Uncle Toma, as I was asked to call him, picked up my haversack and we began to walk together. After a few steps, still sorry to be parted, I ran back to embrace and say goodbye again to Mary and Sanda. It was yet some consolation knowing they would be in the same village. I joined my future guardians and we continued on foot until they stopped by a modest dwelling painted bright blue. The man opened a wicket gate let into the main door and led me through into the farmyard.

"Are you hungry?" asked my new hostess, Auntie Maria. Of course I was, and having said so I followed her to the kitchen. From a small wooden cupboard Auntie took a chopping board on which was a piece of *mămăliga* (maize pudding). She cut a slice and placed the board on the table next to a dish of cheese. I was then left to eat. There was no cutlery so I picked up the pudding in one hand and the cheese in the other and bit into them alternately. When Auntie thought I had finished eating she took me out through the barn into the garden, where vegetables were growing among fruit trees. One tree was full of beautiful red apples, but instead of picking me one, Auntie bent down and handed me one from the ground. Naturally it was worm eaten. She left me with the apple and walked away to pick some stick beans, after which she pulled a few carrots and onions and returned to the house. Once alone I threw away the wormy apple and picked myself a pest free one direct from the tree, eating it with guilty enjoyment.

Sometime later I heard a voice calling me and hurried to find the reason. Auntie was coming through the barn closely followed by a younger woman, dressed in the traditional blouse and skirt, a white scarf wound about her head, fork on one shoulder.

"Lia, this is Olivia, my daughter. She has been working in the fields". The mother retraced her steps, leaving me with Olivia. I stood waiting shyly, not knowing what to say. The daughter was quite slim, and quite old, with bare feet and a plain oval face glistening with sweat. She broke the silence first.

"It's so hot today and I've had the job of turning the hay", she said by way of introduction, in a slow quiet voice. Then she leaned her fork against the side of the barn and picked up a basket.

"Come, Lia, we'll go to collect eggs". I followed her automatically into a dark corner of the barn, checked all the nest boxes, then carried the collected eggs to the kitchen where her mother was now cooking. Olivia began to help with the vegetables.

I put the basket on the floor and offered to peel the potatoes, whereupon I was given a knife. Olivia uttered a cry of consternation when she saw that I held the knife in my left hand.

"Oh, you are left handed, that will never do, leave them for me, you'll cut yourself!" Her reaction did not surprise me, for even in my own village it was considered wrong, even unnatural, to be left handed, and any child found to be so was forced to use the right hand. I am only left handed using a knife, I have no idea why, but hearing Olivia's voice so shocked, I immediately changed hands. At this she smiled, contented that I must be normal after all, and left me to get on with the job. I was much more likely to cut myself now, but that did not occur to her.

Evening came and the table was set for a meal. Auntie Maria placed a large bowl of stew on the table, then brought a steaming dish of *mămăliga*, which she turned out on to the chopping board. Using a piece of string she cut the pudding into slices. We each were given a wooden spoon and while I waited for plates to appear, to my amazement the man dipped his spoon directly into the bowl and began eating. At the sight of his moustache dripping stew down his chin my appetite immediately vanished.

"Help yourself, Lia", said Auntie, seeing that I was not eating. As obviously no plates were forthcoming I forced myself to dip my spoon in the bowl and fish out food from the side furthest away from the man. The stew was very tasty, but the idea of all sharing the same bowl nauseated me. Because I had not eaten much Auntie gave me a cup of milk to finish the meal, which left me disappointed and still hungry, because I had been hoping for some sort of dessert, as in the camp, where meals had always been of three courses.

After dinner, Uncle Toma stood up, wiped his moustache with the back of his hand and went out to check the animals.

It was now quite dark and Olivia lit the oil lamp. Auntie Marie asked me about my family, although she already knew why I was there, and not long afterwards Olivia said, "Come Lia, I'll take you to your bed". There were no sheets, only a coarse homespun cover laid on the mattress, with a rough blanket over. Olivia wished me goodnight and left me in the blackness. In this strange place I covered my head with the blanket and began to cry. I was so unhappy to stay in such a house after the wonderful refugee camp at Daneş.

In the days which followed I saw little of the family, who were in the fields until evening, when we had the meal together. Quite often all three of them would go off early to the work and when this was to happen I would be asked to sleep in the same bed as Olivia, placed on the verandah, because they wanted to lock up the house when they were all out. I did not know whether they had fear of thieves, for surely there was little enough in this poor house for the taking, or whether they did not want me to be left in the house on my own. Whatever the reason, on each of these mornings I would wake to find myself alone, on the verandah, with the house securely locked. There was never anything left for me to eat, so my breakfast and lunch had to be apples and water. I had nothing to do, but as I was afraid to leave the farm, I wandered aimlessly about the yard or sat on the bed. There was never a sign of neighbours, for they too were all out in the fields.

By the time the family came home I was ravenous, yet had some reservations about eating from the communal bowl. The days were so lonely for me now, after having had the company of so many girls, including Sanda and Mary, in the Daneş camp. However, in my bag I still had some of the white material for a petticoat, and I decided to keep it with me on the verandah so that in the quiet lonesome day I could sit and try to finish the garment.

Any interruption was welcome; a passing cart, footsteps, even a stray animal had me running to the gate. In the evenings, when the family came home, there was little companionship for me, Olivia being much too old for a girl of my age to have anything in common, and her father and mother were always engrossed in their farming affairs. I helped with the cooking when allowed, or with other chores, but the period of activity did not last long in the evenings, consisting of having the meal, clearing away, washing up and going to bed.

The days seemed so long to me. Soon I had exhausted my games and I knew every inch of the yard and barn. In desperation I became a little more daring and took my sewing out onto the bench in front of the gate where I could sit facing the road. A little further along another track crossed and I watched and hoped someone whom I knew would pass by. One day, to my absolute joy, my vigilance was rewarded. While picking at my overworked petticoat, slowly and without enthusiasm, at the corner I saw one of the older students from Daneş. Everyone called her Miss Doctor, for she was studying at the school of medicine. Her real name was Marga. I jumped up as though propelled by a spring and called to her, waving wildly. She came along the track towards me, then we both sat on the bench. I was so overcome to see her that I put my head in her lap and began to cry.

"Whatever is the matter, Lia?" she asked with concern, "You have lost weight". She opened my blouse to look at my body and found I was covered in flea bites. "You're only skin and bones, we'll have to do something about that!" I poured out my unhappiness in floods of tears and words, sobbing that I had not seen my sisters, was so lonely, had nothing to do, and, of course, I was hungry.

"Go and put your needlework somewhere, Lia, and come with me to have something to eat", said Marga. I ran back into the yard to throw my sewing on the bed and return gladly to her. Hand in hand we walked slowly through the village, under the heat of the afternoon sun. All the houses looked deserted, with the shutters closed. No one, not even a child, was to be seen.

Marga took me to the home of the priest. How overjoyed I was to see Mary and Sanda again. That day, which had started so miserably, was now filling with happiness. My two sisters were in a good home, Sanda playing cheerfully with the priest's two small children, while Mary did some cleaning and helped with the cooking. The priest's wife cooked me delicious chips and an omelette, then we all had some cakes. Marga told her about my host family, the Borzas, and the lady made a resigned gesture with her hands as though she knew them well, offering to take me into her home if no one else would have me.

I was tearful when the time came to leave , although I now had some hope that Marga would be able to find me a family where I would be more wanted. We went back to the house and sat on the bench outside, awaiting the Borza's return from the field with their cart and oxen. When they arrived Olivia opened the gate to let the animals and the heavy wagon through. Uncle Toma drove the vehicle past, ignoring us, but Auntie Maria came over.

"Who is this, Lia?". Before I could answer Marga introduced herself. "I'm the medical student in charge of the refugee girls in this village. I've come to see Lia, and also to have a few words with you about her". She turned to me. "Go into the house, will you please, Lia?" I did as I was bid. After some minutes Auntie Maria entered the house, dropped the sack she was carrying onto the floor and went through into the kitchen. I heard Marga call out, "I'll see you soon, Lia".

I joined the family sitting at the table. They looked so worn with the days work, dust clinging to their clothes and moist faces. At that moment I felt sorry for them, to have to do so much back breaking work for so little return. For sure they had not been deliberately unkind to me, but it had been a long time since Olivia was a child and they had probably forgotten that children need some attention.

That night I slept in the house, for the following day Auntie Maria would be at home washing clothes. No one mentioned Marga's visit, at which I was pleased for I had no wish to upset anyone.

On the third day after her visit Marga came again and told me to gather up my things, for I was to go with her to another village. I quickly and happily collected my belongings and said my goodbyes to Olivia and her mother, who were at home that morning. I kissed them both and thanked them for having me, took Marga's hand and departed. The two women followed us into the road, watched as we walked away along the track, waved and returned to their work.

Marga and I strolled through the village, then followed a rutted track across the fields until we came to a small cluster of houses. This was Criş, my next village home. We stopped in front of a very high brown gate, upon which Marga banged with her clenched fist. A dog inside began to bark loudly at the sound of strangers. We waited until the clacking of shoes on cobblestones heralded the opening of the gate, revealing a small dark haired, sharp eyed woman in traditional dress.

"Come in, come in", she said smiling a welcome and swallowing something which she had been chewing. "We are just having lunch". Marga and I followed her into the paved yard.

There, beneath a large pear tree, at a table covered in patterned oiled cloth, sat a red faced shortish man with laughing eyes, looking at us from under his crinkled brow. Next to him sat a teenage girl, very pretty, with dark curled hair plaited into pigtails, large dark eyes, black eyebrows and cheeks rosy with the bloom of health. She jumped up and came running towards me, showing her slim well proportioned figure. "I guess you are Lia?", she greeted me with a silvery voice like water in a crystal fountain. She waited for no reply, but continued, "you are to stay with us until school starts. It will be nice to have a little sister now you are here". She bent to kiss me, took my hand and pulled me towards the table. I followed willingly. She hung my bag on the fence, then poured me some water to wash my hands.

"Now, sit and eat, Lia!" In the meantime Cornelia's mother had been trying to persuade Marga to stay and eat with us, but without success as she had already had her lunch.

Then you must have some wine at least", insisted the mother, hurrying into the house and returning with some glasses and a jug. "Made from the grapes of the house, Marga, not strong but just right to drink our health". So saying Cornelia's father handed her a glass, then taking another, he poured a little wine in it, topped up with water and handed this to me.

"Wine with water for you, Lia, to be sure you do not get drunk!", at which all laughed.

I tucked into the delicious food while the others were all talking. They were eating more slowly for each mouthful was interspersed with so much conversation. When Marga finished her wine she came and kissed me, whispering, "Be a good girl, Lia. I hope you will like it here with Cornelia, for she is a nice girl and her parents are very kind people". She sounded pleased to have found me a better home.

Once Marga had left, Cornelia's father stood up and said to no one in particular "The sun is high, I must go and get some of the hay turned before it is too late".

"You, Cornelia, clear the table and wash the dishes, while I go in the garden and do some hoeing", said her mother. I was pleased to be alone with the girl, who quickly cleared the table, poured some water into a bowl and started to wash up. I took a tea towel from the line and wiped the dishes. When the task was completed Cornelia said, "Come, I'll show you our house".

She climbed the steps to the entrance with me close behind. We entered a dark cool room, where Cornelia opened the shutters, allowing the sunlight to flood in. "This is our guest room". I looked around at the two large beds piled high with snow white pillows trimmed with fine lace. Carpets with intricate woven designs covered the walls, except where stood a large chest of drawers fronted by a tall mirror. My guide paused for a moment in front of it, admiring her own reflection. I glanced in the same mirror as I passed by, but the reflection I saw did not make me so happy as Cornelia's had made her. A huge green tiled stove filled one corner. Nearby was a wardrobe and beside it a small table covered with family photographs set in heavy dark wood frames. Amongst them were those of Cornelia in traditional dress, Cornelia in school uniform with a tricolour cravat about her neck, and of the parents at their wedding. The next room, much smaller, was furnished with a bed, a cupboard and a little table. The plain cream walls were decorated with an ikon in red and gold and a small painting, in an ornate gilded frame, of some horses in the evening light.

"You will sleep here, Lia", said Cornelia, patting the bed, "If you get scared on your own, I'll come and tuck in with you". The room pleased me, it felt cosy, comfortable and friendly. I left my companion while I ran and fetched my bag.

Next door was Cornelia's room, decorated in a traditional peasant way, with small red and black towels tied butterfly fashion with ribbons, and pots and plates of painted clay affixed to the walls. A bed, a stove, a smaller wardrobe and a large wooden chest completed the furnishings. Cornelia propped open the lid of the chest and began to take out all manner of items: towels, bed linen, blouses, traditional costumes, belts, tablecloths and much else.

"This is my dowry", she said excitedly. "I am seventeen and I am talking to a boy" (this was the local phrase for courting). I looked at her with childish admiration. To be so pretty, to have a boy friend and a dowry all ready for the day she would be married, what more could there be? After having shown me all her goods she repacked them very carefully, closing the lid with some reverence.

We returned to the verandah. From there I could look down on the village. Pointing to one of the houses, Cornelia said happily, "Over there, in that house with the green roof, lives Peter, the boy I told you about. I can sometimes see him working in the garden and if he looks up he can see me".

After dinner Cornelia took me into the village. By now dusk had begun to dissolve the outlines of the houses. We passed many peasants on their way back from the fields, faces indistinguishable as features became lost in the fading light. There were men and women with tools on their shoulders, carrying bags or baskets, children playing, kicking piles of earth or scattering stones in some game of their imagination. Carts trundled by at intervals, filled with fodder for the animals or small gatherings of crops. As the fires were kindled for cooking the smell of woodsmoke permeated the air, spiced sometimes with the scent of roasting meat. The yellow lights of lamps spluttered and glowed through the shutters of some of the homes.

Cornelia followed the track towards the house she had pointed out earlier as that of Peter. She did not mention this, but said, "I'm taking you to see the church". It was not entirely co-incidental that the way to the church passed close by Peter's house. We strolled slowly, with Cornelia frequently turning her head to catch a glimpse of her intended, but with no success. Eventually we reached the church, simple and unimpressive, roofed in shingles, with narrow barred windows, a short spire and a simple columned portico. The front was painted with biblical scenes now faded in the dim light. Pointing to the building next to the church Cornelia said, "This is the school I went to until I was eleven".

"Is that all? did you not want to go to school for longer? I asked curiously.

"Perhaps, I don't know, but my parents would not have let me. As I am the only child they want to keep me with them here in the village. Another school would have meant me living away somewhere". As we continued our stroll she suddenly began to sing, in her high clear voice;

"My mother says I am
Her very pretty daughter,
And now she will not let me
Go to the well for water,
Not even on a Sunday,
Go to join the Hora
In case I meet a boy
Who will whisk me away!"

The return route took us again near Peter's house, but now two youths stood in front of the gate. Cornelia touched my hand. "Look,

Lia, do you see the two lads? The taller one is Peter". Her steps began to quicken. As we approached the two young men came to greet us. Cornelia, motioning me forward, introduced me. "This is Lia, she is going to stay with us until school begins". The lads looked at me with little interest, all eyes being for the older girl. They chatted for a while about the day's activities, then Peter asked, "The *Hora* next Sunday, will you be there?"

"Of course, I'm looking forward to it", then she paused momentarily and added "But now it's getting dark, we must go".

I thought Peter as handsome as Cornelia was pretty, they surely looked a well matched couple. As soon as the boys were out of earshot, Cornelia asked my opinion, as though it was of some moment.

"What do you think of Peter? Isn't he tall and good looking?" Indeed he was, and I agreed with her, which made her happy and contented.

Back home we found Auntie Anita (as I had been told to call her) boiling the juice for pickling some cucumbers, the smell of dill and onions filling the kitchen.

"Where's Father?"

"In bed, he has to be up at dawn tomorrow to cut the wheat on long hill. Better for you two to follow his example. I shall come as soon as I have finished pickling.

That night I went to bed feeling so happy and relieved to be staying in a good home, with Cornelia and her family. I could hardly restrain myself from exclaiming aloud with joy.

When I woke next morning Cornelia's bed was already made up. I opened the shutters wide and saw the sun well up in the sky. It must have been quite late, I thought, so I washed and dressed quickly. I found Cornelia washing clothes by the well.

"How did you sleep? Did you hear the herd going through?" she asked, smiling.

"No, no, I heard nothing, I slept like a log. Is it very late?" Cornelia glanced up at the clock on the church tower. "It's about ten o'clock. In a minute I'll get you some breakfast. Mum and Dad have gone out early in the fields".

After breakfast she pressed a wide brimmed straw hat on my head. "Now we are off to turn some hay!" She took two wooden forks from the barn, picked up a basket already packed with food and handed me a demijohn of water. We followed a path leading to a field of cut hay and here Cornelia left the food and water in the shade of a nearby ash tree. Some of the hay had been turned and was now rapidly drying in the sun which began to pour heat down on us. The air felt heavy with pollen, and soon a thin coating of dust clung to our faces and clothes. There was no other sound than the swish, swish of our forks in the hay and our laboured breathing. The heat became more oppressive in the still air as the hours passed. Once or twice I heard the bark of a dog, but not for long. Even for the animals it was too hot.

When the sun reached its zenith, Cornelia stopped for lunch. What a great relief to sit and rest in the shade of the ash! I had been very thankful for the straw hat. We used a little of the water to wash our hands before tucking in to our picnic of cheese, sausage, tomatoes, bread and apples. Afterwards we dozed, leaning against the trunk of the tree, but all too soon Cornelia said, "Come Lia, more to do, we must finish the hay before dark". I stood up and looked at the size of the field. Perhaps it was not very big but to me it seemed enormous. Cornelia worked with a rhythm and purpose I could not match. Her lithe body and the fork moved as one entity. Step swish, twist, step, swish, twist she glided along each row of cut grass. I did my best to follow, but soon lagged far behind. The fork was too big for me, so that I had to hold it low, which unbalanced it. My hands were beginning to get sore, but at last I managed to create a rhythm of my own which seemed to please my companion.

By the time the sun was sinking we had finished the whole field. I was hot and sweating, tired, with blistered hands, but so proud. We drank the rest of the water and I walked back, head high, carrying my fork on my shoulder, as Cornelia did, as the others did now descending to the village. The thought that I must look a real hard working member of the community made me very happy. Cornelia again sang softly as we strode back:

"The farm boys are coming into the village,
Singing their songs of working in the fields,
Songs of happiness for they have toiled so hard.
The girls of the village are coming back from sowing,
Sowing the seeds that will grow so tall,
Singing because they have worked so well"

I wanted to sing too, but I did not know the words. I kept silent and contented myself with being such a proud worker.

The church clock was striking eight when we reached the house. In the garden Cornelia stopped to pull onions, potatoes and some beans, saying, "We'll make a surprise for my parents and have the dinner ready for them when they come home".

In the distance bells tinkled, heralding the return of the cattle, and at Cornelia's request I opened the gate to let the animals in. I was a little amazed how the cows, who were collected each morning by the herdsmen and returned each evening to the village by him, always found their way to the correct house. They pushed past, ignoring me. By now I had grown used to them and was no longer frightened, although I treated the long curved horns with respect. Once the clattering hooves had cleared the entrance I shut the gate and hurried back to help in the kitchen.

It was quite dark when Cornelia's parents returned.

"What a lovely smell of cooking" said Auntie Anita, entering the kitchen, then turning to her husband and pressing his arm, continued, "See, Dumitru, when you have two girls much more gets done, even supper is ready and waiting for us". Old Dumitru looked around, eyes twinkling, pulled one of the chairs out from beneath the table and collapsed dramatically upon it with a huge sigh.

"Fill my plate, Cornelia, I'm famished", he said, as the large bowl of soup was set on the centre of the table.

"Go and wash, Father, you'll get nothing at my table with hands as dirty as that", the girl replied sternly. Dumitru raised himself exaggeratedly slowly and with many gesticulations and groans to show his fatigue, he went to the well, washed and returned to his place.

"I saw you two did a good job to finish the hay", he remarked, now waiting to be served, "tomorrow you must pile it into cocks for there could be some rain soon".

The days passed quickly with a similar routine, waking early, working all day in the fields, back home to dinner, then to fall asleep as early as the hens, reminding me so much of the life in our village.

On Saturday the routine altered, the work in the fields ceased earlier and the rest of the day was for cleaning the house and bathing. I was so excited on my first Saturday with my new family, for after I had a bath and Cornelia washed my hair, Auntie Anita said "Come with me, Lia, I want to find something pretty for you to wear tomorrow". All three of us went into the guest room where Auntie opened the huge wardrobe and brought out some traditional costumes. She picked out one, handed it to me, saying, "Here, Lia, try this on, it belonged to Cornelia when she was your age, it should fit you".

With my heart pounding, I rushed to take off my dress, and put on first the heavily embroidered cotton blouse, then the black wrap round skirt, held up with a decorated belt. Cornelia helped for I did not know how the skirt was fastened. Then a black silk scarf with fringed edges was knotted over my head.

"It fits you very well, you look really pretty in that costume", said Auntie Anita, pleased with the effect. I ran to the mirror and there I saw facing me a small edition of a peasant girl of the village. I turned this way and that, examining myself from all angles in the large reflection. "Where is my Mum to see me dressed like this", I said to myself. I was going to be beautiful, a model of all that a village girl should be. Auntie smiled at my obvious pleasure and decided that this was what I should wear for the morrow, the feast day of Santa Maria, and thus dressed I would go to the church and later to the *Hora*. I removed the costume carefully but reluctantly and handed it to Cornelia who wished to iron it.

Next morning I was awakened by the church bell ringing out loud and clear. We dressed in the chosen costumes and walked to the holy building. During the service, in my wandering inattention, I caught once or twice the exchange of glances from Cornelia to Peter, who was standing with his family somewhere opposite us. At last we took our pieces of blessed bread, kissed the ikons and left the church. It was the first time I had seen all the villagers gathered together in their best traditional dresses instead of work clothes.

We wended our way slowly back to the house, where Sunday lunch was soon ready. Shortly after, Dumitru took a siesta, while we cleared up quickly to go to the *Hora*, and by four o'clock we were ready. Cornelia checked in the mirror for the umpteenth time, combed her hair yet again, licked her lips and pinched her cheeks. I could hear music coming from the village square now, and all three of us walked towards the sounds of melody. The road was full of people, attracted by the same magnet to the open space facing the school, where the band of musicians was playing: two accordions, a violin, some cymbals and a piper, going through a repertoire of folk tunes.

Children ran about, excited by the music, groups of friends chatted animatedly, mouths helped by hands, older men and women sat on benches outside houses at the sides of the square, youngsters laughed and joked and practised dance steps. It all brought back more memories of Sundays in my longed for village.

There was an air of fiesta as the band started to play for a round dance and some of the eager youths and girls formed a circle, put arms about each others shoulders and began to dance to the lively rhythm, stepping and thumping feet to the beat, slapping shoes and boots to add to the sound of the dance.

As the lads broke step to run and pull more dancers in, the circle grew so large that a second, even a third ring formed inside the first to give everyone who wanted a chance to join the fun.

The band changed tunes and the dancers followed the rhythms with feet flashing first this way then that, bodies twisting and turning, skirts whirling and flying as each tried to outdo the other in speed and skill. Some of the older generation had joined the circle, moving with great vigour and determination to show the younger set that they were quite capable of keeping up the pace, at least for a little while.

The speed and noise of the music increased, as did the crashing and stamping of feet and clapping of hands. Some of the lads and men shouted out humorous verses to encourage each other to thump out the tempo with even greater energy:

"Turn the girl and back again,
Turn again and stamp once more,
Put your feet down on the floor!"
or
"Stamp one foot and stamp the other,
If you're no good we'll send for mother!"

When the band broke for rest periods the lads and girls gathered into separate groups, with many glances towards each other, and as soon as the music recommenced there was a concerted rush of boys to catch the hand of the girl they favoured most. Cornelia was always one of the first to be taken, but happiest when Peter managed to get to her ahead of the others.

After a couple of hours the number of dancers with any energy left had dwindled considerably, and the exhausted began to creep away to their homes, leaving the square to the fittest survivors. I was taken back to the house by Auntie, who decided that by now I should be hungry, and anyway the cows would be back soon and need tending.

Cornelia's father, who had arrived at the square much later than us, remained on one of the benches talking to some cronies. Cornelia, of course, stayed until the dancing finished and the musicians had departed, but by then I was in bed, recalling the day with mixed feelings; pleasure to see all the people so well dressed and the village full of life and excitement, yet sadness to be so far from home and separated from the rest of my family. Here in Criş I had a wonderful time staying with such loving people and enjoying the companionship of Cornelia. I had no wish for school to start for I would soon have to leave all this joy and again face the unknown.

But there was no choice and inevitably the day of departure came, which meant yet another tearful parting. There seemed to be so many of late. I hugged and kissed Cornelia and Auntie Anita and poured out my heartfelt thanks before Marga took me to the mayor's house. There we were told where we would be sent to school. Mary was to stay in Sighişoara, but Sanda and I were to go to Bucharest.

At the station in Sighişoara there were tears and many words of advice and encouragement from Mary and a last long embrace before

Sanda and I, along with some other girls, boarded the train for the capital. In the crowd of people I saw only the beloved face of Mary, her smile trying vainly to hide her worries. We both waved frantically as the train pulled out and Mary's small figure vanished from sight, leaving me wondering when I would next see her.

SIX

Although the journey to Bucharest was long, slow and tiring, it enthralled me because the train passed through such spectacular scenery. River valleys full of rushing water, sometimes squeezed between the walls of deep gorges. High mountains clothed in the dark green dress of conifers, villages and towns of very different character. I liked most of all the Prahova valley where the train meandered along the course of the river, winding between hills, mountains and houses with brightly coloured roofs of metal or tile perched high amongst the variety of greens.

After the beautiful valley of the Prahova the country became flatter and the towns more industrial, with factory chimneys puffing out black smoke and fumes and much less attractive villages. Around the town of Ploeşti the pungent smell from the oil refinery filled the air. Nodding donkey heads of the pumps were scattered all across the plain and in the distance tall chimneys were sending out great bursts of yellow flame. Groups of ugly grey storage tanks stood near the railway.

As the train crawled slowly towards the main station I could see the devastation of bombing: twisted steel rails mangled in with smashed and distorted wagons, great lumps of broken rusted metal and masses of debris, huge engines squashed and bent as children's toys beaten with a hammer. I stared terrified at such a sinister sight and felt so relieved when the train left the town behind.

Bucharest was the next stop and as we approached the big city there were even more signs of the tragedy of bombing and war. Again the contorted and broken remains of coaches and wagons, large engines half buried in earth, great holes from exploded bombs still unfilled. Everywhere wood, masonry and metal in great sprawling piles. Telephone posts cracked and split, the wires lying on the ground, vicious looking steel teeth of fractured rails thursting skywards. Wrecked houses and buildings between mountainous piles of rubble. How strange and terribly depressing it all looked! Although we had been assured that there would be no more bombing I began to be very scared of going to school in this city.

At the station, which did not seem to be damaged, a great crowd was milling about adding to my feeling of fear as I descended from the train, with Sanda gripping my arm tightly.

Our student chaperone gathered us all into a group, which she led along the platform. After passing the gate she handed us over to a tall woman dressed in Red Cross uniform, who was awaiting our arrival.

"Follow me!" she commanded officiously, and strode off into the throng. We followed, elbowing our way through the crowd, driven by the fear of being lost in such a place. It was vast, with high halls, all crowded, many passageways and entrances with hundreds of people moving haphazardly in different directions.

Doing our best to push through the mass of people we breathlessly chased after the striding woman until finally we reached one of the exits and left the station. The Red Cross woman said, "We are now going to catch a tram. Please keep together and make sure you stay close to me!"

The trams, which came in twos, linked together, were something else new to me. Keeping close to our guide, as directed, we boarded one of the vehicles, which carried us along wide streets lined with huge buildings of solid stone, some grand and magnificent, others, damaged by bombs, had walls and windows broken with mounds of rubble extending into the street.

At the end of the line we descended from the tram and walked to our destination, a military barracks.

After being allocated beds in a dormitory, we were called for a meal and then told that we could go into the town.

"You will stay here until you are sent to a boarding school. In the meantime you are free to go into the town, but be sure to remember the way back, and please do not be late for meals".

Left to our own devices Sanda and I spent our time exploring the streets of the neighbourhood. At first we were afraid of becoming lost in this overwhelmingly large city of streets and buildings, so utterly different from anything in our village, but I rapidly became used to finding my way.

After three days of such exploration we discovered a very beautiful park, which gave us a great deal of pleasure. There were plenty of trees, bushes, flowers and greenery and a small river leading to a huge lake, so many ideal places for playing hide-and-seek. Little humped back bridges spanned the stream and on the lake many wooden boats floated, available for hire. In this very large park we spent most of our time, for there was so much to see, so many paths to run along, so many people to watch. Quite a few had dogs on leads, trotting alongside the owners. These dogs looked so pampered and well fed, very much unlike our rangy village dogs. I so enjoyed the park, which was like a little paradise for me.

We had no idea when the schools would start or to which one we should be sent until the morning when John came unexpectedly to see us. It was such a wonderful surprise. After our effusive kissing and embraces he said joyfully, "Let's go to a cofeteria and have some cakes".

I had seen the cake shop during our walks. It was a large room furnished with tables and chairs where people ate whatever they had bought at the long shop counter. The confections lay displayed in a glass cabinet. Often Sanda and I had pressed our noses against the shop window to look at those tempting, mouth watering goodies, but we had no money to go inside. This time we entered boldly, following our confident brother. As always, he was impeccably dressed, now in light grey trousers, with a pale blue shirt which emphasised his bronzed skin.

"Choose what you like", he said grandly, waving his hand towards the display. It took both of us quite a long time to decide on such a delicacy. There were cakes of all shapes and sizes, all so attractive, of cream and jam, of chocolate, of thin pastry wafers and more with fruit. At last we made up our minds, to the relief of the other waiting customers and of the serving girl, who was gazing dreamily at our tall handsome brother.

We sat at one of the tables and ate our cakes slowly, savouring the creamy sweetness of such a treat. John let us all finish, and while Sanda sucked her sticky fingers, he said.

"I've really come to see you because I have some good news. I've arranged for you to go to a very good school. It's called the Eleana Doamna orphanage. There are about four hundred girls there, so you'll have plenty of company".

"But we're not orphans, why can't we go to a proper college" I objected immediately.

"Oh, Lia, you should know why. Who is there to pay any fees or accommodation for you? Anyway there is no other school where you and Sanda can be together. Moreover, it was the Ministry of Education that told me where you are to go", he admitted reluctantly.

"Do we really have to end up in an orphanage?" The very word had such a final ring to it, and somehow sounded degrading. I was almost in tears.

"Cheer up Lia, it's only a name. It really is a very good school and you are lucky to have got places there together". I was not so sure about it, John had a way of turning things to his advantage.

"When do we go there, if we must?"

"That's why I am here. We'll go back to the barracks and get your things, then catch a tram directly to the new school".

It did not take us long to gather and pack our few belongings before journeying to the orphanage. The tram stopped near a pair of large iron gates. We descended and John opened one of them for us to enter a spacious garden, mostly green lawns. Further back stood an imposing long two storied building. Near to the main porticoed entrance to the edifice was a stone pillar with a bust of the founder of the orphanage mounted on top. When we came closer I read from a plaque, "Eleana Doamna". "Who was she?" I asked.

"She was the wife of the first King of Romania when it became a united country in 1859", replied John to my question. Up some steps at the entry the porter directed us to an office where a bespectacled woman with ginger hair asked us, in a bored voice, what we wanted. John approached her and in not much more than a whisper said that he had been sent there by the education authority, handing her some papers in confirmation. The woman took them into an adjoining office. The door soon re-opened to admit another middle aged lady with a severe looking face and straight grey hair, wearing a well cut grey costume. She spoke irritably to John.

"Very well, you can leave your sisters here, even though we are so overcrowded with many girls from Bessarabia and Bucovina. Let me have your address in case I need to contact you in emergency."

Minutes later a short dumpy barrel of a woman entered the office. She wore a grey skirt straining at the waistband and a white blouse. Her hair, parted straight down the middle, was plaited into two pigtails coiled on top of her head. Her florid face sat square on her thick shoulders as though she had no neck. I did not like her one little bit.

"Come with me, you two girls!" She commanded in a deep voice.

Both Sanda and I clung to John, not wanting him to leave us in the hands of such an amazon, but he said. "You must go now with this lady. Be good girls and I'll come to see you again as soon as I can". Reluctantly we released our hold on him and, left with no alternative, we followed the stumpy woman, who turned out to be our matron, through a long high corridor which had a floor of ceramic tiles polished like glass. There were many doors each side of this passageway. Up by a twisting staircase to the next floor we persued the matron's clacking shoes. She stopped at one of the doors, opened it and revealed a huge dormitory, with four rows of beds placed next to each other in pairs, all in perfect line. The matron pointed to two which had only mattresses on the iron frames and said abruptly, "You will sleep here until terms starts". Apart from a screen in one corner which partly hid another bed, a wardrobe and washbasin close by there was no other furniture in the room.

The matron went to an open window and shouted loudly.

"Duţescu! come here immediately!" In a few minutes a schoolgirl entered, clad in the uniform dress of small navy and white checks, topped with a navy pinafore and starched white collar. She looked about my age and was panting breathlessly.

"Take these two sisters to the cloakroom and tell Mrs Popescu to give them bedding and show them where to store their things". She stomped off leaving us in the care of Duţescu. For a moment we looked at each other mute, then she picked up Sanda's bag and marched through the doorway. We followed along the polished corridor.

"What's your name and where are you from?" she asked of me, but without waiting for a reply continued, "Got anything to eat? Sweets or anything?" Hearing that neither of us had even a crumb, she made a grimace of disappointment. With the confidence of familiarity Duţescu led us down staircases and into a dark corridor. Reaching a hidden door she knocked and waited. The sound of footsteps from within preceeded the door being opened by a small white faced woman, slightly stooped, dressed in black. After greeting her the girl repeated the message from the matron and ran off, leaving us to enter the room. We were in a large basement, the walls lined with shelves divided up into small compartments, each with a number painted on the front. Most contained layers of clothing. The little woman sat at a desk, took a dossier from the drawer and registered our names within.

"You", she stated, looking at me, "will have the registration number 323 and you, Alexandra, will be 255. She pointed to the compartments with the corresponding numbers and told us to deposit our belongings within. She checked to see that we had three changes of all underwear and it took but a glance to see that our trousseaux were far from complete. She calmly produced the extra garments from a cupboard and made up our deficiences, then gave us each a needle and a hank of red thread to embroider our numbers on the clothing. After taking away our bags she finally piled our arms with two sheets, a blanket, pillowcase, towel and a nightie.

"Go upstairs now and make your beds", she instructed in a small calm voice. Just as we left the store, loaded with the bedding, Duţescu arrived, still breathless. I was pleased to see her, being otherwise sure that without her guidance I would have lost my way in the maze of corridors and passageways. She watched critically as we made our beds, and when satisfied she led us into the school grounds, which were quite extensive, with trees dotted near the edge of the grass. Tables and benches sat between the trees. Many girls of all ages between six and eighteen were around, some playing games, others reading or chatting. A few sat on the steps of the chapel attached to the main building, while several rested on the grass or benches, one or two knitting. Seeing newcomers, a few came to inspect us curiously. One asked what form I was in and, hearing that I was the same age as her, offered to show me round the school. Sanda, unwilling to be parted from me, came with us.

"I'm Alexandra Comănescu", the girl introduced herself.

Behind the chapel a wooden fence separated the orphanage from another building, a training school for primary teachers. A high stone wall bordered the long side of the garden.

"Bet you can't guess what's behind this wall?" queried Comănescu.

"No, what is it?"

"It's the Palace of Cotroceni, where some of the Royal Family lived"

As we walked alongside the school building our guide pointed to some windows, set low down.

"Here in the basement are the kitchens and the shower rooms. We can go through the chapel to get into the main building". Once inside, Comănescu showed us the ground floor classrooms, and the dining room. Upstairs, through windows still plastered with crosses of brown paper, I could see over the magnificent grounds of the palace. We walked along the upper high corridor until suddenly Comănescu stopped, drew in her breath and whispered fearfully.

"The matron, come quickly, we are not supposed to be here in the daytime". She turned to run, but was much too late.

"What are you girls doing here?" boomed out the loud voice of the dreaded woman. "Comănescu, come here right away!"

We stopped in our tracks as if frozen to stone. The matron marched up to us, shoes echoing on the tiles and slapped Comănescu full on the face. She turned to me, grabbed a handful of my hair and banged my head against that of Sanda.

"You have only just arrived and already you are breaking the rules, now get outside!" We hurried down the stairs, heads ringing. Instinctively I had not liked the woman from the beginning, now I positively hated her. How did we know what the rules were? It really was unfair.

"I would like to push her down the stairs!" said Sanda, sobbing and rubbing her head.

Shortly afterwards the chapel bell chimed aloud and the girls began to rush for the entrance. We joined in automatically, through the big doors, along the corridor and into the dining hall. In a few minutes the benches were filled with pupils who obviously knew their places. Sanda and I remained standing, uncertain of where to go.

"You two!" someone shouted. "Go to the table at the end, in the corner". We did as we were ordered and found ourselves at a table for twelve. One of the girls hurried to an adjoining room and returned with a large bowl of soup which she ladled into metal plates and passed to all at table. At this point, the matron, who seemed to be everywhere, made a gesture to us all to rise and recite the Lord's Prayer before sitting down again and scooping up the soup, which was a thin watery concoction laced with a few small pieces of carrot and onion. When the plates were empty the duty girl collected the main course from the servery, and once again served us all. This was *mámăliga* and cheese, but so little, merely two spoonfuls of the pudding and one of grated cheese.

"Is this all we get?" asked Sanda, unbelievingly.

"I suppose so, perhaps the sweet will be better". I turned to my neighbour and asked. "What do you think will be for dessert?" She gave a derisive snort.

"Dessert? You'll be lucky to get any here, even when it's a special day, and there aren't many of those".

After the frugal meal all were sent once more into the grounds, until the bell tolled the signal to go to the dormitories. It was nine o'clock. I watched what the older inmates did and copied them. The uniforms were laid carefully over the bedheads so as not to crease. Then, with nighties on, the girls went to the washroom, situated at the end of the corridor, to wash feet and clean teeth. There were rows of washbasins, back to back, fed by a single pipe suspended above, taps supplying each basin. Then back to bed. At ten o'clock the matron switched off the lights.

After a day of so many changes I could not easily sleep. Thoughts of my family and my village tormented me. Every move I had been forced to make seemed to take me further and further from all that I loved and yearned for. Firstly Dad, then Mum, then our home and village.

Now my three brothers were so scattered I had no idea when I should see them again. Luckily Mary remained in Sighişoara, where her entire school had taken refuge, so she still had some of her teachers and friends. Basil was studying in college in Făgăraş, Constantin, my appointed protector, was sent to Beiuş. How upset Mum would been if she had known that her plans for us had gone so awry. John was now in the medical school in Iaşi. At least part of his dream was coming true. I recall him showing his hands one day to Ephraim.

"Just look how long and delicate my fingers are, not like yours", he said derisively looking at the hands of his half brother, calloused with hard work. "I shall be a doctor, I think, perhaps even a gynocologist with hands like this". Ephraim, having no time for the fancy ideas of the boys, who in his opinion were just workshy, replied by throwing a basket at John.

The more I thought about home, the more heavy hearted I became. It was so dreadful to think of the forseeable future in this orphanage, where everything seemed so spartan and disciplined. I tried to hold back the tears and reached over to touch Sanda, in the next bed, to seek some grain of comfort from her presence. I worried about her as well, whether she was homesick or distressed.

The next morning at seven o'clock everyone wakened to the loud unmusical clanging of the chapel bell. I jumped from the bed as though scalded, thinking of Comănescu's warning of the previous day about being ready for prayers.

"No one better be late, that's certain punishment!" Sanda and I were already used to the headlong rush routine of getting dressed and making the beds, but today we were extra careful to get it absolutely correct. New to us was the system of staying in twos in the corridor until the matron called on some girls to leave the column and say prayers. These must have been written by someone in the school, for they were tailor made to fit.

"Thank you, Lord, for bringing us to this school where we have everything: clothes, shoes, food and education. Give, Oh Lord, good health to the headmistress and the teachers . . . rest in peace all the donors of money who helped build the orphanage: Eleana Doamna, Anna Davilla, Carol Davilla, Eleana Proca (the list went on and on)." I utterly disliked this so called prayer and never succeeded in learning it. Consequently I always feared I would be asked to recite it. Usually girls with good diction were called for the readings, but there was the possibility that some slight lateness or noise would bring me to the attention of the virago and I would be selected. I so longed to be back home.

From the day after our arrival until the school term started the main task was to clean the wooden floors in classrooms and bedrooms with pieces of broken glass. We worked on each parquet block, first wetting it then scraping away with the glass until all the old polish was removed. Whenever left alone, our frenzied scraping, which sounded like a thousand mice in a big brown cupboard, eased off to a near stop. As the cleaning ended, the dust was swept up and the polishing commenced. This was a little more pleasant, at least our knuckles were not so sore, but still a hard job, for the floor had to be polished to the shine of patent leather shoes. All of us were on our knees rubbing madly away at the floor until it reached the required standard. At least, while anyone was watching. As soon as the matron left the room, a method that someone had thought up or learned from somewhere was used instead. One girl sat on a folded blanket on the floor while two others dragged her from one side of the room to the other, as on a sledge. This was much more fun and very effective, with a lot less work. Of course we had to have a lookout for to be caught so flagrantly disobeying the rules would have meant a punishment. As soon as the sentry's stage whisper "Matron" reached our ears, the blanket was hidden away and by the time the dragon entered all of us were innocently polishing furiously with the pieces of cloth.

Another time the matron would order. "Now take all the blankets and mattresses outside for cleaning!" Everyone, including me, groaned, for we all detested this. Beating the dust out of the bedding was such a dirty job, even if it was considered necessary.

One more task was that of making the tomato juice. In the kitchen hundreds of tomatoes were chopped into small pieces, which then had to be boiled for a long while. Between the chopping and boiling, when no one was looking, as a slight compensation we were able to slip some of the pieces into our hungry mouths. The boiled pulp had to be strained to get rid of all the skin and pips. Then the glutinous red juice that remained was boiled again in huge pots, with the contents being stirred the whole time to prevent burning. I hated this part because in the heat of summer, standing by the pans, stirring the steaming liquid with large wooden spoons, was absolute torture.

How much I longed, at that time, for the school to start properly, when we should only have to study! In September the term finally began. Hundreds of girls arrived for the start, adding to the numbers of those who had stayed at school over the holiday period. This first day of term was quite exciting with so many girls greeting friends and aquaintances after the vacation. Everyone avidly studied the notice boards to check the dormitory they would be in and which classes they would attend.

The gardens, which had been fairly quiet in the previous weeks, were bursting with excitement and bustle with so many newcomers. Each class of about twentyfive to thirty pupils had a dormitory to itself. Sanda, still in the primary school, was no longer beside me, which was sad, although in a way I thought it better for her to learn to be independent, for she had been relying on me a great deal in recent years. In the new school uniform, with her hair combed tightly back into two bunches she looked different, no longer Mum's little angel, but a quiet and melancholy girl.

There were three sections in this orphanage: Primary, Secondary, where general subjects were taught, and Senior, where the fifteen to eighteen year old girls spent most afternoons in practical lessons of cooking, spinning, weaving, knitting and art projects as part of their training. This was aimed at fitting girls to be good wives, for as all were orphans or poor it was thought by the powers-that-be that the best hope for such a girl was to make a good marriage. Sometimes we heard very happy stories of pretty girls from the orphanage who had been chosen by wealthy or important men as wives. For me this was not all that attractive a future although it sounded an easy way of life.

I thought it much more important to train first for a career, not depend on the luck of a happy marriage.

Now, at the age of twelve, I entered the Secondary section. The first teacher I encountered, the wife of one of our most famous painters, was a very jolly lady, fond of telling jokes. It was a relief to see someone smiling and joking, after the sadistic matron!

The rest of the teachers varied in their approaches to us. The one with the most notorious reputation for being a tartar was the maths mistress. When she entered the classroom with her grey streaked hair drawn tightly back into a bun, her steel rimmed spectacles and severe no nonsense black dress I could well believe it. From the beginning she asked me questions about my work of the previous year, but after all the things that happened to me it was difficult to remember much. She declared herself very dissatisfied with my knowledge, yet was completely unhelpful. Because she was so strict and her attitude so unkind, I became quite an adequate failure at maths for that year.

School term started with discipline well to the fore. In the classroom, just before lessons, the door would sometimes crash open. In would march the matron, wooden rule under her arm, staring petrifyingly at everyone.

"Hands on the desks!"

All hands were smacked palms down on the wooden tops. The owners waited, trembling, while she passed slowly along the lines, inspecting nails and one's general appearance.

"What's this black under your nails, Comănescu?" Smack, smack went the flat of the rule on the unfortunate girl's knuckles.

"You, Coman. Late up, were you? No time to comb your hair properly". Under the nets we had to wear, a lock or two of her hair was peeping. This the matron would pull vigorously, and as an added bonus slap the attached head against any nearby wall or blackboard.

I hated and resented that awful woman, and wished her dead many times, but I learned very quickly to do everything correctly so that I kept out of trouble. However, I think it affected my personality for I became more passive and reserved.

In the dormitories we had little white bags, tied to the bedheads, in which we kept our toilet things. These were a prime target for inspections. Toothbrushes and combs were hauled out and minutely inspected for specks of dirt and toothpaste, both punishable offences. The white collars of our uniforms had to be washed each day. There was no way of ironing them, so to stiffen them they were soaped and stuck to the wall. When dry they became as stiff as though starched.

Soap was in short supply and the smallest pieces were saved and put in a muslin bag, which was then tied and used to wash with.

The navy uniform pinafore had three pleats either side of the front and these had to be pressed perfectly. The common method was to arrange the dress carefully on the mattress, replace the sheet slowly on top, then sleep on it. How difficult it was to rest, trying not to disturb the pinafore beneath!

All the matrons felt free to join in the inspection game. Passing in the corridor one would say "Take off your shoes!" If there were holes in your socks, woe betide you, another offence committed. One of the punishments meted out for a hole in a sock or some equally terrible crime was to be stood in the dining hall, facing a pillar, with the offending article pinned to one's back. For some girls this was quite a traumatic experience, but for those who were less sensitive or more cheeky it was an opportunity for a show of bravado in front of their colleagues. As the matron passed by, the offender would make faces, or put her tongue out at the woman's back, promoting an outburst of giggling.

"What are you girls laughing at?" The matron would demand, but by then the miscreant would have straightened her face and be staring fixedly at the 'Pillar of Infamy.'

As a reaction to the severity of the staff the girls themselves were usually kind to each other, some of the older taking the younger ones under their wings, and teaching them most of what they knew about the facts of life and how to cope with the problems of puberty. I was very naive at the time and eager to learn all I could about the mysteries of sex.

One evening an older girl brought a book into the dormitory to teach us about this. With a well briefed lookout at the door, we all crowded about the 'teacher' and her book. As we were about eleven or twelve, we found it difficult to understand anything seriously and in embarrassment were giggling and making silly exclamations. After the older girl left we let our imaginations run riot, with some girls attempting to play the part of the man as they understood it. When one of the demonstrators tried to lie on top of another girl 'to show how' there was an immediate protest from the partner beneath. "That's horrible, get off, you're squashing me, you must be stupid, I think the whole thing is awful!" I myself was left more confused that ever and decided it best to leave the subject for later, there were many other pressing problems to cope with in the orphanage.

Nowhere else did the days take so long to pass as in this place, with the time between meals becoming interminable voids. As most other girls, I was always so hungry that the long hours seemed to fill up just waiting for the next meal. Being so soon after the war, supplies were severely rationed. Meat, butter and cheese were rarities, and tea was merely water coloured with burnt sugar, often tasting and smelling of something else as the cauldron was not used for tea alone.

Breakfast consisted of a cup of the hot sugared water and a slice of bread which had been quickly looked at by some jam. Occasionally, if we were very lucky, we had, instead of the jam, a thin scrape of peanut butter. Lunch was a well watered down soup and a stew of lentils or leeks. For dinner a slice of maize pudding and jam, or sometimes a little cheese. Then it was time to do homework, which was sheer torture, for all I could think about was food.

How much I longed for some sort of celebration day, such as the Saint's day of the Queen after whom the school was named, when we were given a little more to eat, but there were not many of these welcome days.

When these occasions occurred all of us gathered in the so called 'Hall of Donors' to listen without much interest to the speech of some important personage or other. My gaze wandered to the hanging portraits of famous people who had donated money to build the orphanage, such as Eleana Doamna, Anna and Carol Davilla, etc., and I thought they were looking down on us with a mixture of pity and kindness, or perhaps it was only my imagination playing tricks.

On Sundays there were no classes and relatives and friends could come to visit. Almost always they brought gifts, perhaps no more than a piece of bread, or one or two eggs, but something.

I can visualise even now the school on these days, with the lucky girls who had visitors walking and talking with them at the front of the building, usually happily eating a treat which had been brought, while girls such as Sanda and I, with no relatives around, stayed on the first floor above, looking down on the lucky ones with envy and mouths awater.

Even though we made the best of it and tried to put on brave faces, I for one was sometimes in tears that the two of us had no one to come and see us in the first years and bring us some little tasty thing. Looking down on the happy group below I sometimes fantasized that my parents were coming through the gates, dressed as they were when they went to church, Mum in the velvet dress and Dad in his best suit. Then they would be sitting on one of the benches, with Sanda on Mum's lap and me on Dad's knee. We would, of course, be eating one of Mum's scrumptious cakes. It was just pure imagination, but how I yearned for a visitor, anyone, to come and bring a ray of sunshine into the day.

Some of my classmates were kind and occasionally gave me a piece of fruit or a sweet they had received, which I had to rush to Sanda with and share. Quite often I spent the Sunday with her, helping her with homework, or combing her hair. If it was a fine day I would often sit on the grass and let her lie against me with her head on my lap. I felt so close to her and so protective, for she seemed very young and fragile.

Our morale was pretty low from the cold unloving atmosphere and the lack of food and vitamins. Ulcers began to break out on our legs, which was due to malnutrition, but I did not know that. Sanda was affected more than I. She looked pale and drawn, with her straight blonde hair accentuating her pallidity. We were given some awful smelly ointment to put on the sore places, but it did not do much good. What did help us, but not appreciated at the time, was a large bottle of cod liver oil sent to me by a Miss Slivici, who had been on the Refugee Committee and remembered Sanda and myself. I thought that nothing could taste as horrible as that spoonful of oil each day.

Luckily, a year later, in 1945, the two of us were chosen, with others, to go and spend our summer holiday in Bran, where the Commissariat for refugees had opened a camp for girls like us. I was so happy and excited!

We made the trip by train in which two coaches had been reserved for us, with plenty of seats, not as my first train journey from Kishnev. The village of Bran was situated in a beautiful mountainous area, partly forested. Horses and carts took us from the nearest station to the camp, which was once again a village school.

It was late and dark when we arrived, and after a meal and hot milk, Sanda and I went to bed in a room with nine other girls.

The excitement of being in a new place kept me awake for some time. I was so anxious to see the castle I had been told was there. As dawn broke I crept into the corridor in the hope of catching a glimpse of it and, lo and behold, there it was, a magnificently impressive fortress perched high on a great rock, surrounded by conifers. How eerie but majestic it looked in the morning light!

I heard someone coming and ran back to bed, not knowing the rules in this place and not wanting to do anything wrong.

There were a prince and princess and their six children living in the castle, and I tried to conjure up visions of them. Would they be as handsome as the princes and princesses of some of the stories I had read? And what could it be like inside the castle? Fantasy worked overtime for me.

A bell interrupted my thoughts. It was time for the washing, and bed making routine. After a delicious breakfast there was an assembly during which we were introduced to each other and told the daily programme. As we were free for the rest of the day I ran immediately out of the camp to see the village. Opposite our school a small river was spanned by a wooden bridge which led to a hutted barracks. There I saw many injured young men, some walked slowly with the aid of crutches, some were with arms in plaster, others with bandaged heads and a few sat in wheelchairs. I guessed these must have been soldiers who had fought in the war.

I headed towards the castle, along the river, looking everywhere with curiosity and interest. Further along I came to a pretty little footbridge. Crossing it and following the path brought me to a beautiful tiny church, half hidden by trees. It was such a peaceful spot, carpeted in long grass, liberally sprinkled with wild flowers.

At the end of the path I discovered a monument, a large rock in which an opening had been cut and framed with marble pillars, the front protected by a decorated metal gate. Inside sat a marble chest partly covered in purple velvet. I learned later than in this quite modest place was the heart of Queen Mary (a niece of the English Queen Victoria). The story went that she had requested, when she died, her heart was to rest in the little chapel of the Royal Palace at Balchik, near the sea, where she had been so happy, and the casket containing the heart layed on a plinth covered in her favourite material, dark purple velvet. However as Balchik had been incorporated into Bulgaria in 1940 the monument had been moved to Bran.

The few houses scattered along the river bank looked to me very elegant and beautifully maintained, most of them being used by the rich as holiday homes.

Now my greatest wish was to see the princess and her children, and to this end I spent much of my time around the castle. My vigil was soon rewarded as the splendid iron gates were opened and a nanny, dressed in pale blue, with a white apron and bonnet, came into the garden, accompanied by five children, a boy with short leather trousers as worn by Austrian children, and four girls between the ages of four and twelve. I could not stop staring at them, for the girls were so pretty, with long blonde hair and superb dresses, the smallest skipping along, two other sisters holding hands, while the eldest stayed back a little emphasising her seniority. The boy, about six years old, was playing with a ball. I could not see him clearly enough to scan his features.

A car stood in the drive, with a chauffeur waiting by the open door. The five rushed to take their seats, pushing and jostling as all children do. The nanny sat beside the chauffeur and they drove away. A motor cycle followed the car, driven by a very good looking boy perhaps fifteen years old. I heard later this was the young prince Stephan. Afterwards the motor cycle, I think the only one in the region, was to be seen often in the village.

The next day, about nine in the morning, a knot of people gathered about the bridge which led to the barracks.

"What's happening?" I asked a woman dressed in the local costume.

"Princess Ileana, from the castle, is coming to make her daily visit!" Minutes later a car drove up and the Princess emerged. She was dressed in a nurses uniform, similar to that worn by the hospital staff, but in much finer material. She turned and waved to the bystanders, smiling warmly. I looked at her with curiosity and admiration. She was in her early forties, tall, with large blue eyes, dark brown hair covered by a very fine scarf of woven silk in place of the nurses bonnet. Her face was slightly tanned, emphasised by the white headress. Once she entered the hospital I wandered off.

The camp life was as wonderful as in Daneş, with plenty of appetising foods and interesting activities. One day the head told us we were to sing for the Royal Family living in the castle. This was such a fantastic event and we worked hard to be ready, practising our repertoire each day. Finally, on the appointed day, after dark, we walked quietly to the castle, carrying torches of burning pine wood. Grouped near the part of the castle where the bedrooms were situated, we started to sing. The atmosphere was ethereal, the blended voices sounding as a chorus from heaven. The flickering light of the burning wood reflected on our faces and hair. Scents of the surrounding forest perfumed the gentle breath of the night.

Shortly after our serenade began the windows opened one by one and in the yellow torch light we could see the heads of the Prince and Princess and those of the children. When we finished singing the main doors of the castle opened and the whole family came out to stand silhouetted against the interior lighting. The scene was as one from fairyland, absolutely unforgettable.

Later that holiday the Queen-mother Eleana and her son, the ruling King Michael came to visit the castle and the barracks hospital. Formed in two rows we waited impatiently, as did all the locals dressed in their beautiful costumes. Preceeded by the police escort the royal car passed slowly by, giving us all the chance to see the Royal Family. I had seen only their portraits previously, but now here they were, real, and in front of my eyes, smiling at us. We waved little flags or threw bunches of wild flowers in front of the car, which drove quietly to the castle.

The following day, Sunday, the Royalty were to attend service in the little church near the castle. The King and the Royal Family walked the short distance. I looked at him in wonderment, so tall, slim and handsome in his beautiful military uniform. After the service all made their way to the shrine where Queen Mary's heart was entombed, laying large wreaths on the monument. It was such a happy day for me to see these almost legendary figures.

While in Bran we had the chance to go and see the competition for the prettiest peasant girls in traditional costumes made by themselves. This took place in the next village, one of the judges being the Princess, who herself gave prizes to the winning girls. The beautiful costumes, true works of art and design, were worn by girls who looked so pretty and blooming with health. At the end of the contest the boys joined them for rounds of folk dancing.

One day the Princess visited our camp. We worked hard to make the place look festive, with many ropes of flowers hanging from the ceiling. The table was covered in dark red velvet and decorated with arrangements of wild blossoms.

The princess entered smiling and walked round the room, touching the chin of one girl, stroking the hair of another, asking names. We performed a little entertainment for her: songs, poems and short dialogues. Everyone was so overjoyed that a Princess came to visit the camp and say kind things to us! We learned later than she had given us some hundreds of metres of cloth to have dresses made.

The castle held an endless fascination for me. Every evening as the light began to fade, the edifice would take on a mysterious brooding appearance bordering on the unreal, almost supernatural. I thought often of the various kings and queens who must have lived there over the centuries. One of these was Vlad Ţepeş-Dracul. His portrait from my history book came to my mind, with his aqueline nose and cold strange eyes. I would have been frightened of him, I am sure, yet in spite of his appearance we had been taught that he was a good king of Transylvania, who, inheriting a kingdom riddled with corruption and crime, did something about it. His rather drastic solution was to have a spear driven through the body of any felon. It was said that in a surprisingly short period crime had disappeared.

I did not know at the time that he was the subject of Bram Stoker's book of the legendary evil vampire count, and I wonder whether it was his looks, or his method of punishment that caused him to be chosen for the story, and I have no idea where the vampire came into it.

As with all good things, our marvellous holiday came to an end and we had to return to Bucharest, but the summer camp had been a great blessing. I hoped I had eaten enough of the plentiful good food to set me up for the coming year. The physiques of Sanda and I had changed dramatically, our thin pale bodies having fattened out by several kilos, our cheeks were now painted in healthy colours and the sore places had healed.

I hated the idea of returning to the spartan conditions of the orphanage, but had no choice. My great hope was that I might be selected each year for such a summer camp. Sanda and I were luckily picked for the next year, 1946, but this was to be the last time.

Great political changes, which we knew little about, were going on in the country. From the time Romania had pulled out of the war, in 1944, the government, under Russian pressure, had been growing more and more communist. The prime minister had been shot as a fascist sympathiser, and in the December of 1947 King Michael would be forced to abdicate and leave the country, along with the whole Royal Family.

We were no longer regarded as refugees and the camps were disbanded. In 1948 a Soviet type constitution was proclaimed and from then on the Communist system tightened its grip on the country. For me it meant that any future holidays would be spent in the orphanage.

To this day I recall the time after the abdication of the King, when Romania became a Socialist Republic. We were told to tear from our schoolbooks all photographs and pictures of the Royal Family, and everywhere their portraits were torn down.

Being young, naive and quite isolated politically as a schoolgirl, I did not really understand what was going on, but I did notice that not many of the staff were happy about the changes. They showed their disapproval with small actions and gestures. After an inspection to check that all royal pictures had been removed, one of the teachers wrote on the blackboard 'Viva King Michael'. The maths mistress, seemingly completely out of character, came into the class, unbuttoned her cardigan and from a pocket withdrew a picture of the King. She kissed the portrait and said "I'll keep him here always", and patted the pocket near her heart. Many others expressed openly their displeasure at the new regime.

I felt affected only when the time came to study languages. Until now the older girls had all been taught French, to which I was looking forward, but to my disgust this was now abandoned in place of Russian. I so envied those girls who had learned French for six or so years.

Now, in the classroom, in place of the Royal portraits were hung those of Gheorghiu-Dej, the new president, and of the group of four; Marx, Engels, Lenin and Stalin.

SEVEN

In 1949 the orphanage closed down and the building was altered to become part of the University. Some of the pupils, including Sanda and me, were transferred to a new school, specially designated to train teachers of infant children. I was extremely happy at the change as it put an end to the severe discipline and cold atmosphere of the orphanage.

However, in later years I admitted that I had learned a great deal there, both educationally and about life in general. The discipline had been a good force in our upbringing. A number of true friendships had been formed that lasted for many years after. I myself met several girls who had completed their education before the orphanage closed and they all had made good marriages and were happy with their families.

Before leaving the orphanage the bursar gave me an envelope containing my documents and school reports to be handed on to the new school. Being inquisitive I opened the envelope and checked the contents. I was absolutely petrified when between the various pieces of paper I found a certificate proving that my parents had been deported by the Russians to Siberia. If such a document was accepted and useful in 1944 when people were very sympathetic towards those who had suffered the loss of their homeland of Bessarabia and whose relatives were taken to Siberia, by now in 1949, with the new regime dominated by Russia and run by Russian sympathisers, any document proving the deportation of one's parents was a terribly incriminating thing to have.

With my heart pounding madly I rushed to the toilet and tore the paper to shreds before flushing it away. Sanda did the same with her piece of paper and I thanked God that I had been curious enough to open the envelope.

In the new school, which was much smaller, with only one hundred and twenty girls, all between the ages of fourteen and eighteen, I had the feeling of being in a large family. Everyone, including the staff, were so friendly, and the two matrons were both much kinder than any we had previously encountered. The food also was a vast improvement, with the cook at times asking us what we should like her to prepare. Probably it was easier to run a smaller institution now, some years after the war. Moreover, in this school most of the girls were not orphans, but had parents who contributed to its upkeep.

As the school courtyard was too small for games or exercises we were taken several times a week for a walk in a nearby park. I enjoyed these outings very much for they gave me the chance to see a little of the town life.

Opposite our school was a Polytechnic with many boys, who soon began to figure more and more in our thoughts. They rapidly became a magnet for the older girls, who by some means rapidly invented a sign language with which they managed to communicate with the male students.

Shortly after we moved to this new school a ball was organised, to which the Polytechnic boys were invited. Everyone was so thrilled at this prospect, for most of us had never before had any opportunity to meet boys socially. For the occasion we were allowed to wear whatever clothes we liked. There was a period of frenzied borrowing and swapping of dresses and shoes until we were all satisfied with our outfits. In the evenings, with the aid of a gramophone lent to us by the matron, we tried desperately to learn how to dance, a few older girls being the instructors. It was a time of feverish excitement.

The day for the ball came and we all entered the decorated hall and sat on a row of seats, chatting animatedly and wondering whether any boy would ask for a dance, and if so, what would he be like. Never having danced with a boy before, I was so nervous that my hands were shaking and my knees were like castanets.

The boys, all smartly dressed, came in small groups, standing for a while near the entrance, looking furtively at us girls until the music started. Then they all rushed to invite the girls who had taken their fancy. Three of them came towards me. I was too flustered to be flattered, but one was a tall fair boy I had seen glancing at me, so I chose him. He introduced himself to me while I was doing my best both to avoid walking on his feet or falling over. When the first dance finished, instead of walking away, he held my arm until the next began, a waltz I think. I floated now to the melody. I could dance, and here was a good looking boy dancing with me, *with me*. I could sense that he liked me. I danced and danced in a daze of enchantment, changing partners at times, but often returning to the fair boy. Occasionally I caught a glimpse of the teachers standing by the foot of the stairs smiling at us youngsters enjoying ourselves. Sanda was dancing too and as we passed each other in the rounds of the dance I saw happiness glowing on her face, something which I had never seen in the orphanage.

Too soon the ball had to end, but my memory kept the fair boy with me through the night. I could feel his arm about me, his hand in mine. I looked for him often in the days that followed, as the Poly students passed our windows on the way to their classes, and saw him a few times. All we could do was smile and wave at each other. I never met or danced with him again, but the memory of that ball lingers yet.

The move to this new school was a blessing for us as it coincided with Constantin and Basil coming to Bucharest to study medicine, and they were able to visit us quite often. I was very proud of them when they came on Sundays, both now six feet tall and slim. I caught many a glimpse of various colleagues staring at the good looking young men and I soon became very popular with many requests for introductions to my two brothers. Constantin was especially attractive to the girls, with his clean cut features, green eyes and thick dark curled hair. He had a greater aura of sexual awareness than Basil, who still had a bland innocent face. He was slightly loose limbed, with hands that seemed more suitable for farming than doctoring, but his kindness and gentleness made up for any other shortcoming. Both wore military uniform, which added to their glamour. They had accepted entry for some years into the Medical Corps as it was the only way they were enabled to study medicine and be provided with accommodation, food and clothing, for they had no assets and no money.

Mary came to Bucharest a little later to read physics and mathematics, so was also able to come to see us. She was now a well developed young woman of nineteen. Her frame was a little larger than mine, and with her almost black hair, large brown eyes, dark eyebrows and apricot skin I am sure she had quite a following of male admirers.

Sanda had grown too, she was taller than me but at fifteen still thin and rather flat chested and annoyed about it. Her hair was blonde as ever and rain straight, but she had beautiful deep blue eyes and dark eyebrows. Her personality had developed, she was stubborn at times and not at all as ambitious for a career as was I. Infant teaching suited her, as she loved young children about her, and I felt sure she would be quite happy with marriage. She had now a natural grace of movement for which I rather envied her.

A few times all six of us managed to be together, with John making the trip from Cluj, where he was a senior medical student with just one year of study to go. He was as debonair as ever. Now at twenty seven, tall as the other two, he was well built, broad shouldered, with a near perfect body, thanks to his devotion to exercise and sport. All traces of boyishness had left him, but he was still jocular, optimistic and careful to enjoy his freedom and escape any marriage vows. As fastidious as ever in his dress, looking always as though he had just emerged from the tailors, he would parade in front of us, head up, chest out, cocky as a pouter pigeon.

"What do you think of this coat (or suit or whatever), doesn't it fit me well? What do you think of the material?" His bonhomie brightened us all, so that we forgave him his fault of being so often secretive. No one ever knew how he had managed to get the money to be able to study in the civilian medical school, an impossibility for the other two brothers. He made vague references to a grant but how or why we never found out.

However, it was a magnificent day when we could all be together.

We would find a quiet spot in the park, sit and talk over our plans, hopes and dreams. Those very happy years were as a credit on the balance of life, evening out much of the periods of hardship we had previously experienced as children.

The eternal sad note was the continued absence of our parents. We could only hope that they would survive and that one day we should see them again. The very first time all of us met after the orphanage years I posed the question to John.

"Have you managed to find anything out about Mum and Dad yet?"

"No, not yet".

"Couldn't you write to George or Ephraim, maybe they have had some news?"

"Lia, you have been out of touch with reality for years in that orphanage so you cannot realise the danger of writing to anyone back in our village. Let me explain now we are all here. Not long after we left home as refugees the Russians started to demand that all the people who had fled from Bessarabia should be sent back. I was simply too terrified to write and give my address to anyone in the village, thinking that the security police would come for me, then probably for all of you".

"Couldn't you have asked the International Red Cross to help trace them?"

"What, you mean write to Geneva? What chance do you think any letter of that sort would stand to get out of the country? All letters sent abroad are censored, and it would have been a sure way to get into trouble. It's just not possible yet to do anything."

Basil butted in. "You don't know what happened to me in Fágáraş in 1946. One day two of my classmates came to me in a panic.

'Quick, Basil, you must hide', they said, 'Some men are looking for boys from Bessarabia!' In a minute I was crouching in a cupboard behind some boxes. I stayed there for ages until it was all clear. Even though it turned out the security men were looking for two boys belonging to a family unlucky enough to be sent back to Russia, I was scared for ages after!"

"You see Lia", continued John, "with such things happening who dares to write, perhaps to risk our lives for a letter? On the other hand we don't know what is going on in the village, if George and Ephraim are still in Slobozia, and a letter from me would endanger them. After all, they are also father's sons. All I can do is promise that whenever it's possible to contact someone in the village I will do so."

With that explanation, unsatisfactory as it was, I had to make do.

Every time we met and walked together through the streets I was conscious of people turning to stare at us. "Look at them, they must be brothers and sisters, their parents will be proud of them", someone whispered at the time.

The love and affection which existed between us six gave us all such a wonderful feeling and made up for any lack of material things. My heart glows even now when I think how Basil, at sixteen, being very good in his studies, managed to earn a little money by helping younger boys with their lessons, and with the earnings he sent us whatever he could find in the way of supplementary food, as well as stamps and envelopes so that we could reply to letters. I was delighted for him when he came first in his class. He won several prizes, mostly books, for his efforts.

During one holiday, before he started medicine, he worked so hard cleaning old bricks by hand, in filthy dusty conditions, in order to gain some cash. Generously, when he visited Sanda and me, he asked what would we like as a gift and we chose some knee length socks for winter. At the next visit he brought our coveted socks. What I did not know then was that at the time inflation was so high the purchase had cost him nearly all his earnings for the whole holiday period. He was always kind and helpful and such a generous boy.

Then Constantin, while at college in Beiuş shortly after the war, wanted to come to see us during the Christmas holiday, but had no money for the fare, so he took the job, in bitterly cold weather, of selling butter in the open market in Bucharest, because travel to and from the capital was thrown in. He was also able to bring us a pack of butter, more precious than gold! Such gestures of love are for me unforgettable.

In his letters Constantin urged us to study hard, and impressed upon me that the only way to avoid the misery of poverty was to concentrate on my work and get good marks. This stimulated my efforts a great deal.

During the two years I spent in the training college, although enjoyable, with the opportunity to see my brothers and sisters fairly often, I came to the conclusion that teaching infants was not for me. I wished to end my learning years with a much better qualification than being an infant teacher, and that meant I should have to get into University.

I had been interested in the life of plants and animals since a little girl and the fact that our recent biology mistress had the gift of presenting her lessons in a very attractive manner made me think that biology should be my subject.

I finally made up my mind on a holiday which all six of us were lucky enough to spend together. Basil had a friend whose father was a priest, and he invited us to spend the summer holiday in his house which was situated in a very picturesque region near Făgăraş. From the house we could see the peak of Moldoveanu, the highest in the country. It was a challenge and we decided to climb it.

After miles of trekking the forest gave way to high grassy slopes with small stunted bushes, then the grass thinned to leave only barren rock for the final stretch. The last hundred yards were by far the hardest part of the climb, being almost vertical.

We scrambled to the top, breathless but victorious, overcome by the wonder of the panorama before us. It was a clear day and I was higher than any other living thing in the country. I had been told that the Danube could be seen from this peak and in the far, far distance I saw a steak of silver as from a mirror. If it really was the great river or just an illusion of mist I did not know or care. For me it was the mighty Danube, the romantic river which, from a spring in the Black Forest, crosses or touches eight countries before discharging into the Black Sea. Below us the pine forests swept away in billowing skirts of dark green, their petticoats of lighter greens and yellow peeping beneath, to be edged with the lace of tiny patchwork fields and hedges. Here and there flashed the sequins of little streams bouncing in ribbons to the feet of the hills.

I felt that there could not be any other moment for me of such supreme happiness, and understood then what was meant by 'See Naples and die'. I had the feeling of nothing being able to surpass this perfect beauty of untouched, unspoiled nature. If I had died at that moment it would have been worth it just to have stood there. Impressed with the awesome scene I knew right away that I would have to find our more about all this wonder that surrounded me, all the marvellous art of life. My decision was made on the spot, I would be a biologist!

Our holiday continued pleasantly enough, but never attained that pinnacle of delight again, and all too quickly I was back into the usual college routine.

At the first opportunity I told the principal that I wanted to apply for entry to the University. She immediately poured cold water on my enthusiasm.

"You cannot do that until you have passed your exams and worked as a teacher for three years". This was a bitter blow and I felt dejected, but I decided not to take *NO* for an answer. I would appeal to higher authority!

I went to the Ministry of Education, walked through the main entrance and told the receptionist that I wanted to see the Minister. He looked at me with some astonishment, but directed me to an office.

"What can I do for you?" asked a secretary, eyeing me disdainfully.

"I want to see the Minister", I replied naively.

"That's impossible, he is a very busy man. What is it you want with him, anyway?"

After I explained to this prim and proper madam, she said. "You have already spoken to your principal and she gave you the correct answer. There's nothing I can do!"

I burst into tears, so frustrated by this reply. However, the good Lord must have been on my side that day, for as I was booing my heart out, the door opened and in came the great man himself. He asked me, quite kindly, what was the matter, and I dried off enough to explain that I was an orphan and had worked so hard to get good results. I had not asked to be put in a school for infant teachers, and wanted to get higher in life than that, but no one would help me.

"I will have to see what I can do for you", he said sympathetically. A few days later I was called to the Principal's office.

"You can apply for entry to the University as soon as you have finished your baccalaureate. This is quite exceptional, you are lucky to have such a chance and I hope you make the best of it".

This was wonderful news, which gave me the drive to study hard every spare moment. After sitting the exams for entry I had to wait several nail biting weeks until the results were posted. As soon as I heard they were on the board I rushed, with my heart beating madly, to look. There it was, my name on the list! I was in and could now look forward to my dreams coming true.

EIGHT

A few days before I finished my studies at University I had a very long letter from John. My heart began to race when I reached the paragraph saying that he had recently received the fantastic news that our Mum and Dad were alive. After almost two decades of deportation to Siberia they had been allowed to return to Slobozia where they were now living with Ileana and Ephraim in the old house by the river, our own house having been taken by the state for use as a village hall.

I read and re-read John's precious letter many times to make sure my eyes were not playing tricks with me and each time my whole being was warmed with this wonderful glowing feeling. Tears came to my eyes but this time they were tears of happiness. I began to wonder how *Mama* and *Tata* would look now. I could visualise them so clearly as they were before the deportation, Mum, rosy cheeked and full of vigour and youth, Dad tall, strong and slim, with dark curled hair. But how would they be now? Old and ill? Broken by the years of hardship? Perhaps prematurely aged? Deep in my heart the love for them stood undiminished by time.

At the end of his letter John asked me to write to Mum and Dad as they were so anxious to hear from us all, and eagerly awaited our letters.

It was now possible to write to my parents as after Stalin died in 1953, the deportations virtually ceased and people, once they lost the dread of being sent to Siberia on any pre-fabricated excuse, became confident enough to communicate once again.

How could I start the letter to my parents? What could I write after such a long period of uncertainty, during which my heart had always hoped for their return, but my logical head held the fear that by now they must be dead?

My sense of euphoria at the marvellous news was soon tempered by worrying thoughts crowding into my mind. All letters, especially those sent abroad, were still censored. If it became known that I was no longer an orphan, but had parents who had been sent to Siberia, what would happen to me? I did not know what to think so mixed and confused were my feelings.

During my years at University I had studied hard and diligently to get the highest marks I possibly could. I obtained excellent results in my exams, and had even been awarded a Republican grant, which very few students gained. Because of all this I had been accepted for a job as an editor in Bucharest, where I was due to start after the summer holidays. But another important criterion for the job was to have, in the Communist party jargon, 'a healthy background'. As an orphan, my background was untraceable and accepted, but now, out of the blue, my situation had dramatically changed. I was no longer an orphan, but the daughter of parents who had been deported to Siberia, and if this terrible slur became public knowledge in this twisted repressive totalitarian state system, I should immediately lose my job, and probably count myself lucky if I was only sent to some remote village to teach infants.

Fuelled perhaps by adversity my brothers, sisters and I had worked so hard to get decent careers, and now, at least for me, it could all count for absolutely nothing. It was certainly an ironical twist of fate, that the return of my parents from Siberia, for which I had prayed for so many years, could now result in my own downfall. Appalled by such a prospect I decided to do nothing for a while until I had time to think more about the situation.

The summer holidays came and I spent part of it with Mary, now an attractive cheerful young lady, already married and a teacher. One weekend there was a reunion of us all at her house: John and Constantin, both now doctors and both married, Basil, still a bachelor, again a doctor, and Sanda, a teacher for infant children.

We embraced each other, overflowing with happiness knowing that our parents were alive and back in our native village. Nostalgically we reminisced over our childhood in Slobozia, once more becoming those little boys and girls of the happy times. We sang songs, one of which brought me to the verge of tears, thinking so much of my Mum and Dad.

"Why did you bid me part with you
Why did you let me go?
I wish I had remained a ploughman
With scythe and spade and hoe.

On tortuous paths in foreign lands
I would no longer roam,
and at your age now, you would have had
a helping hand at home.

After my service in the wars
I would have settled down;
My wife and I would have been farmers
of credit and renown.

The many grandsons you could have had
To call you grandmama
The many stories you could have told
about good times and bad.

With endless prayers, you poor old folk,
Your days drag on, ne'er cheered,
and mothers tears fall on the psalter,
and father's on his beard"

I took the opportunity of this reunion to talk over the situation regarding my job and the re-appearance of our parents after everyone had accepted us as orphans, and to think out what to do. It seemed so ridiculous that any of us should suffer from the deportation of Mum and Dad, and we all agreed that it was not right or just to go again through any periods of trauma for some stupid political ideology, and if the truth was to affect our careers so much, then it would have to be tailored.

After the holiday I proudly started my job in a prestigious institution, with offices in the most imposing building in Bucharest. I soon got used to my colleagues and managed to make some friends. The working atmosphere was very pleasant and I felt, after a little while, that people liked me. This helped me a great deal to summon up the courage to tell them about my parents.

On the crucial day, hiding my nervousness, I burst into the office with a beaming smile on my face.

"Why are you so joyful this morning, Lia?"

"How could I be otherwise when yesterday I had a letter from John with the marvellous, and unbelievable news that our parents are alive, not killed in the war as we were told".

"That's just incredible!" Everybody agreed.

Stimulated by the questions which were then fired at me, I told them the story my brothers and I had thought out previously. "In 1944 when many people were running away from Bessarabia our parents did the same and brought us to Iaşi. Once we were settled with some friends, Mum and Dad decided to return home for some more possessions but while they were there the border was closed by the Russians and my parents were trapped without warning. That was the last we heard or saw of them until now. All six of us were then sent to some refugee camps, as the friends could not keep us for ever. When school started we were separated, Sanda and I being sent to the orphanage here and the others were scattered in four different towns where their schools had taken refuge from Bessarabia. We were unable to see each other for some years, and only sporadically write when someone gave us envelopes and stamps".

Discussion of my story lasted most of the day, with very little office work being done. The news soon spread through the whole section and whoever I met in the corridor fired questions at me. I felt a little guilty with my partly invented story, but with the exception of the details of my parents everything else was true. Later that afternoon I went to the records office to have my dossier updated and my tale was accepted without comment, much to my very great relief after so many nights and days of tormented thoughts and fears.

Then happily I wrote my first letter to Mum and Dad. It was extremely difficult to condense all of what had happened in seventeen years into a few written pages, so I selected carefully only what I considered interesting from my life as a schoolgirl. I wrote about Mary and the brothers and a lot about Sanda with whom I spent so many years in the same schools, about the happy times when we could all meet as students, and stressed how proud I was when walking together to see people turn and look at us, three tall handsome lads and three joyful sisters. Deliberately I left out the difficulties, but was enthusiastic about my interesting job and what I did with my first salary. I slipped in a photograph I had, a copy of the one on my diploma.

John had already written to them and asked for an official invitation. Without such a document none of us would be granted passports. The formalities to get permission to visit our parents took, in all, three months, but at last we had the passports in our hands and the date of departure fixed for our summer holidays.

Loaded with suitcases we took the train for the USSR and after a six hour journey reached the border. There passports were scrutinised, baggage minutely searched, questions asked, but finally we were cleared and the train clattered across the bridge spanning the river Prut. What sad memories this river brought back to me of the time when I had last crossed it, nearly two decades ago! On Moldavian-Russian soil the train stopped at Ungheni, where everybody headed for the border post. Here the checking again took an interminable time, then we waited another hour or so until the train for Kishnev came.

Once aboard I stood transfixed at the windows, gazing nostalgically at the countryside of my childhood; the low hills, green fields, vineyards and woods, villages and small towns. All seemed so new for me now, unable as I was to remember anything from the last trip as a little girl.

In Kishnev most of the buildings were modern and so monotonously alike. A statue of Lenin dominated the main boulevard, now alive with people of many nationalities, all so unfamiliar to me. Still John and Constantin could recognise some of the older buildings from their days spent at college in the town.

"Look at Sobor cathedral, the cross has gone. I suppose the Russians have transformed it into something else. Lenin's monument certainly did not exist. What have they done with the statue of Stephan the Great? And look at the street names, all are now in Russian!"

Basil went off to find out how to get to Slobozia, and returned with the news that we had missed the only bus of the day. He suggested we go by taxi. I cannot forget the Russian driver, who drove his Volga as though the dervishes were after him, ignoring all the potholes in the road, swerving and swaying around everything in his path.

When we passed though Kiperceni John and Constantin competed excitedly with each other in recognising landmarks and pointing out the differences between what they now saw and what they could remember.

Butterflies fluttered in my stomach when we entered Slobozia and approached the old house where our parents were now living. I was curiously disturbed to find that I was unable to recognise much of the village, in spite of the driver going now very slowly because of the twisting tracks and the need for directions. As the Volga chugged along the once familiar route, I thought of the child I had then been when I left Ileana and Slobozia in Toma's wagon. How narrow the track had become, just room for the taxi to squeeze by, yet as a little girl it has seemed so wide! When we arrived I stepped from the car with the blood pounding in my ears, my breath coming in gasps. My legs felt like jelly and almost refused to hold me upright, so overwrought was I with emotion.

The noise of our arrival brought two elderly figures to the door of the house. We dropped our cases and packages and rushed to greet them, our *Mama* and *Tata*. They were trembling visibly, both crying yet trying to smile. Mum held the handrail for support, one hand on her heart, and stood speechless for a while, then came to hug each of us in turn with such force she was shaking, and kissed us noisily on each cheek. Dad did the same, after crossing himself two or three times, trying to control his tears. Then Mum stepped back to look at us again. Poor soul! it was heartbreaking to see her forcing herself to recognise her own children after such a long parting.

"Surely you are Lia?" she said, her face lighting up. "I remember that small scar you have on your cheek, but how much you have grown'" She then threw her arms around me and we both burst into fits of weeping. She soon recovered a little and stared at us all once again, saying, "And you surely are Sanda, with your blonde hair? Oh, my little angel, how much I worried about you, you were so young when I was deported". Then she held Sanda and kissed her many times. Parting from Sanda she looked again at us as though we might disappear any moment. "Oh, dear children, you have all grown and changed, but you are so tall and thin! Obviously anyone can see you had no one to look after your properly". More tears streamed down her cheeks.

"I have to thank God with gratitude for giving us the chance to see each other again after so many years", said Dad in a husky emotion laden voice.

I looked at the two of them, my Mum and Dad, and for a moment they were strangers to me, so old and worn. There was nothing left of my happy young Mum and the tall handsome Dad I remembered. The dreadful years in Siberia had turned Dad's black hair into grey whisps and robbed the flesh from his body. They also had faded Mum's joy of life and added many lines to her aged face. Only in their eyes was there a flickering warm flame that struck a chord within me. I do not know how many times they made the sign of the cross, how many times they thanked God for keeping them alive to see us once more.

I peered about the yard where it had all began so many years before, then forced my eyes up to look at the house where I had been born. How sad it all seemed now, yet in those former years this place held so much joy, happiness and love. Everything had changed, everything had shrunk. The old house looked so low, with such small windows and a door through which my brothers had to duck to enter. Inside, where all was neat and tidy, my eyes scanned anxiously for some familiar thing, any small item that I could recall, but there were none. Everything was so modest, so altered from the images my childhood memory had left me.

When Mum spoke again I sensed that she could hardly comprehend the irony and injustice of it all, to come from Siberia and live not in her own farm, but in the old house which Ileana and Ephraim had been using as a store shed.

"Look where we live now. My very soul is torn apart when I go into the village, pass our farm and see our lovely house transformed into a village hall, where the useless wretches who are in power hold their stupid meetings!"

"Come, now Nicola, do not upset yourself. We should both be grateful God helped us to return from that awful Siberia", said Dad, trying to stop Mum becoming too upset in telling of her pain. "Anyway, now with you all here the yard is coming to life again!"

After washing off the grime of the journey we sat cheerfully at the table, with Mum at one end and Dad the other, as in the old days. The large table was set with mounds of mouth watering foods, but before we ate Mum insisted we said grace. The meal was as delicious as I remembered through all the years. That, at least, was unchanged. After a few glasses of home made wine raised in toasts to each and all of us, John, with his irrepressible sense of humour, tried to create a jolly atmosphere. "You are not doing too badly, Mum and Dad, look here, plenty of food and wine and a roof over your heads, what more is there to want?"

"Thank God we are here and have enough to eat, but it is still terribly painful to think we have lost everything we worked for all our lives. The two of us manage with what we get from the collective and that is because luckily Theodore works hard, otherwise we would have very little", replied Mum sadly.

"What do you think I do now?" asked Dad, without expecting an answer. "I am a watchman for the calves and have to spend all my nights sleeping on a plank in the barn to be sure no one will steal the little creatures. How respected I was once, and now I have a job fit for a clown".

Mum had suffered for some years from heart trouble and could not do much in the collective, but from time to time she was given no choice but to work stringing tobacco leaves, for which she received a mere half the dole of the rest of the workers.

While sitting around the table I often caught Mum's deep green eyes looking at us intently, as though she was trying to find a connection between us and the children she loved so much and had been forced to abandon.

"Why are you staring at us like that, Mum?" asked Mary.

"Because I'm just not able to take my eyes off you, my dears, after so long. I can't get over the way you have all grown up and changed so much."

After the meal we spent hours around that table talking about the village, the relatives and aquaintances, our childhood, the war and a myriad of other subjects.

Ileana and Ephraim came in, tired after work, to renewed emotional embraces and tears. I hurried into Ileana's open arms as I used to when I was a little girl and she was looking after me. "If you didn't have that little scar I could hardly recognise you", she said, stepping back and studying me from top to toe. Both she and Ephraim had not changed much in appearance, I thought, they were still young, just at the age Mum and Dad had been when they were deported. I was terribly upset to hear that none of Ileana's family had ever returned from Siberia and she obviously still felt the loss very deeply.

Then Ephraim shocked us with his war stories. At first he was on the side of the Romanian and German armies fighting against the Russians, but later, when Romania pulled out of the war and Bessarabia was handed to Russia, he returned home, only to be conscripted again, this time into the Russian army to fight against the Germans. The young conscripts from Bessarabia had a cruel fate in the Russian army, soon being sent to the front lines around Berlin. The fighting there was horrific, Ephraim and his comrades had to walk for miles over dead and wounded soldiers, mostly Russian, hearing and ignoring the screams and cries of those needing help. Very few of Ephraim's unit survived, but those who did, including him, were decorated for their bravery in the battle for Berlin. Now he was only a tractor driver, working long hours in the vast fields with the ever present fumes and noise of the diesel engine.

"George was much wiser than me", he said, "for he gave up his farm and ran away with Marika to another village, miles from here, and so escaped any fear of deportation, but myself, ever since I came back from the war, have been living in a kind of nightmare, being constantly insulted and persecuted as the son of a *Kulak*. Only the medals the Russians gave me for bravery have stopped me being deported to Siberia as well.

I realised that Ileana's personality had changed dramatically from the gentle person I knew. She was now bitter and spoke roughly about the wives of the collective's bosses who did no work but stayed at home and looked after their children, while she, with three little boys, had to work hard in the fields or spend all day stringing tobacco leaves. "All the lazy good-for-nothing thieves and vagabonds are doing very well under this crazy system. Some are foremen, some are supervisors and bosses in spite of being as stupid and useless as ever, but they think they are gods".

Next day we all strolled through the village. How small everything had become. It was as though I stepped from memory into Lilliput! The river, which had scared me when I was five, where my daring brothers had played and splashed us girls, was but a little stream, flowing quietly and humbly under the plank, still there as a bridge. The church, which had played such a prominent part in our lives on Sundays and feast days, looked now insignificant, dull and neglected, with a rusted door which had remained closed for years, the churchyard overgrown with tall ragged weeds. In this regime only the older people dared to go to services, and they had to travel to the next village where there was still a priest and an open church.

The imposing school building which had so impressed me as a child I would have now passed without a second glance, and the huge yard had dwindled to a mere patch of threadbare grass.

I began to feel apprehensive and the pressure in my chest mounted as I approached our farm, my brain still confused by the images of the past which could find no parallel with the here and now. I looked around the courtyard which used to be our playground. The sheds and the cart on which we had played as a seesaw had gone, as had the hayloft where Constantin liked to hide and read. I sat for a while by the front gate, staring mournfully at the unkempt front garden, choked with weeds. Slowly and reluctantly I raised my eyes to the house. It was distressing to see it now uncared for and semi-derelict, with dirty windows and broken stairs. The verandah fencing was rotten and hanging in pieces. The thatched roof had been replaced with corrugated iron, already rusted. The cellar still existed, but neglected and empty. A small house had been built in place of the barn, but the people who lived there were strangers I had no wish to meet. There was no mulberry tree, no orchard, no beehives and no stork's nest. It suddenly struck me that I had not seen such a nest in the whole village. "Where are the storks, Ileana?"

"Oh, my dear Lia, they have been gone for years. When these new roofs were put on to do away with the thatch all the nests were destroyed. I was so upset the next spring to see the poor birds flying round and round the village trying to find their homes. In the end they all flew away. They will never return, they can't build nests on corrugated iron, can they? No, no, Lia, the storks will never return to us in this village".

I felt so dejected to hear such a story, for the storks had been very much a part of my childhood life, and so much of a legend. They only nested, I had been told, on the homes of good people. How eagerly I had searched in my innocence to find those houses not favoured with a nest, and beware of whoever lived there.

But no more.

I pitied the village children who would no longer see and hear the arrival of the elegant storks, with their clacking beaks, watch them rebuild their great nests, teach their youngsters to fly and follow their migrations in the autumn.

With a heavy heart I left the farm which had once been so precious to us all, and walked from the village to see where our fields had once been. On the way we passed a heap of rubble.

"Remember the farrier?" asked Ileana, "this was his place". Memory came back in a flash. When our horses needed shoeing Basil and I would go to the farrier to see the fun. We stood at a respectful distance, watching the craftsman hit the white hot iron with his great hammer, jumping each time he dipped the hot shoe in water with such a loud hiss of steam. He was a short, red faced man with a huge black moustache, wearing a shiny black leather apron, tied about his middle like a band of armour. He loved to tease the children who came to watch, and we were not exempted from his jollity, especially if we ventured a little too close.

"Ah ha", he would say, turning his ruddy face towards us "you want to be next, do you? I can make shoes for boys and girls just as easily as for horses. If you want I'll fix you up after this animal!" Then we would move a little further back, just in case he meant it.

But now nothing was recognisable. In the fields the boundaries had gone, the small farmlands joined now to grow huge areas of tobacco and maize.

"Over there used to be our vineyard" said Dad, pointing in the direction of a sea of tobacco plants. Dotted about on what was left of the meadow, where the boys practised riding the horses, stood ugly corrugated sheds housing the animals of the collective. Even the yellow clay pit had been filled in and grassed over, for the material was no longer used, having been replaced with concrete.

This bitter sweet day of confrontation between memory and reality affected me deeply. Everything reminded me of our dashed hopes and lost happiness. I now felt an outsider, a stranger in my own birthplace.

"Things do not seem very well kept in the village, don't people work so hard now?" asked John, looking around thoughtfully.

"Work hard? No one works hard here, they have no idea what that means. I used to start at sun up, four or five in the morning, you remember, but now they all begin with a meeting at eight o'clock to decide who does what! No wonder all these collectives are so inefficient, you've seen the state of them. But, I'll tell you a little secret. If I had been as conscientious as I used to be I probably would not be here now!"

"What do you mean, Dad?"

"Well", continued my father, "I'll tell you. One night last winter it was really bad, the wind howling and the rain lashing down. In the barn, with the calves, lying on the plank, I thought no one is going to come out tonight to steal any of these creatures, I'll take the chance and go home for a decent night's rest, which I did. Next morning when I went back to the barn I found that the roof had been partly demolished in the storm. I looked inside to see if the calves were all right, and there, on the plank where I had rested, lay a great beam fallen from the roof, right across where I would have been! So it looks as though being conscientious does not always pay!"

The next day we all visited Auntie Alexandra, Mum's best sister in all the world. She was now elderly but tall and erect as ever. I would have recognised her soft voice and laughing eyes anywhere, even after those years of separation. Never did I think that one person could give so much love and care as she had for us when our parents were taken. Next to Marika and Ileana, she had been our mainstay without whom I am sure we would not have survived.

Theodora, the cousin who showed me how to roll down the hill, was now in a house of her own, married and with six children. I found it difficult to see, in this thirty year old mature woman, the girl of ten with whom I had once played so often.

Mum insisted that we visit all our relatives and friends. She and Dad were proud to show us off as having made good with our lives despite the deprivations we suffered when we were young.

Those days in Slobozia stirred so many memories and emotions, revived moments of happiness, sadness and pain, hope and success, and as they drew to a close we asked more and more questions about Mum and Dad's time in Siberia. At first they refused to talk about it, fearing to spoil our marvellous reunion, but under so much pressure from us they eventually agreed to tell of their terrible ordeals in that far off hell.

NINE

"It is so fine and warm today, let us stay in the garden under the walnut trees", proposed Dad. "You, John, go and fetch some wine from the cellar, it will help ease the heartache of this Siberia you want us to tell you about".

When we were all settled Dad put an arm gently on Mum's shoulder and said, "Nicola, I'll leave you to begin as I think I need some more wine before I can face telling my story".

"Oh, God", murmured Mum, sighing deeply, hand pressed to her heart, "I hardly know how to start".

"Maybe with your detention in Kiperceni, when we brought you the quilt", suggested Constantin.

"All right, I'll try, but it is so awful to think about. Let me see . . ." she paused as though collecting her thoughts. "Yes, after a couple of nights in that NKVD place I was taken to the prison in Orhei and pushed into a stinking cell with some other women. It was just ghastly, with damp stone walls, a concrete floor, bars like a cage, and a barrel cut in half for a toilet. I was so depressed I could do nothing but cry and pray. The fear that they would have taken you children as well continuously tortured me. Next day I was told that I had been sentenced to five years imprisonment for being a *Kulak*. Five years in such an awful place! I thought I would die worrying about you all, about Dad and the farm. I don't think I shut my eyes for days.

That quilt you brought me was a real blessing, for at least I did not shiver at nights as some other women, who were taken unprepared and had only thin summer frocks.

After many days spent in these horrible degrading conditions I felt exhausted and could do nothing else than passively accept my cruel destiny of staying there for five years. But it was not to be so, for one day, unexpectedly, we were marched out of the prison, put on some carts and taken in the direction of Kishnev. I had no idea why or to where we were being moved."

Here John interrupted Mum's tragic story. "I know why. The Germans were attacking the Russians, and the Romanian army, on the German side, was advancing into Bessarabia. That began on the twenty second of June 1941, a date I'll never forget, for the Russians who came here in 1940 to Russify the region were forced then to leave in a panic, but not before they retaliated barbarically by scattering petrol in the most important buildings and setting them on fire. Whole streets were gutted in Orhei and many other towns. When Constantin and I came to look for you, Mama, the prison was wrecked and some of the buildings were still smouldering and smoking. I can smell even now that peculiar reek of burnt buildings and rubble". John stopped there, allowing Mum to continue.

"Well, anyway, in Kishnev we were marched to the railway, split up into groups of about sixty prisoners, men and women, and forced into filthy stinking cattle trucks, the doors slammed and bolted behind us. The only light we had came through a small barred opening high up. Some dirty straw littered the floor and in one corner a hole had been cut to serve as a toilet. There was not enough room for us all to even sit down properly. I can't tell you how terribly frightened we all were. No one knew what was to happen to us, they gave us no food or water.

Shut in the wagons people reacted in different ways, some crying and praying, some sobbing in fear, but many just stood dazed as if in shock. After some while the train moved off and travelled until we reached the Dnistru (the river border between Bessarabia and Russia). We knew where we were because from time to time some men climbed on each other's backs and looked through the little opening.

As the train crossed the iron bridge over the river there was such a terrible screaming roaring noise, followed by great explosions and the sound of guns firing. The train was being attacked by aircraft. Pieces of shrapnel and bullets tore though the wagon sides, with everyone in panic, screaming and shouting in their fright, but the train kept going. Something chopped into my leg and cut it badly. I don't know what it was, probably a piece of metal. I tore a strip from my petticoat and bound the wound to stop the bleeding. Many others were crying and groaning for some had been badly hurt and several killed. Hours passed before the train eventually stopped and the doors were opened.

We were on a siding. Some men tried desperately to get out, but the guards stopped them, pointing their rifles, "Anyone gets out will be shot". Then they ordered us to push out the dead, leaving the wounded with us, without giving them any help at all. There was little we could do for them, for we had nothing.

Then the soldiers pushed in some buckets of water and flung dry grey bread at us as though we were dogs, before shutting and bolting the doors once more. It was a real fight, scrambling over each other to get a piece of bread and a drink of water. The journey went on and on for many days. I lost count completely. What with the stench, the hunger, fear and the shrieks and groans of the wounded I thought I would go mad. Each time we stopped the dead were cleared out, for quite quickly the wounded and some old or sick people began to die. But there was no more room, for as the dead were thrown out more prisoners were forced in to make up the number.

Sometimes we were left on a siding for days, still shut in, often without food or water. Some of the people really went mad before they died. One day two men forced apart the bars of the opening, in utter desperation, and climbed out. As they crawled through the hole some soldiers sitting on the roofs of the wagons shot them down. After that incident the opening was nailed up with pieces of wood, so then we only had the light and air which filtered through the cracks between the boards.

Most of the guards were very sadistic and cruel. On one occasion those devils in uniform gave us some dried fish. As I was starving I rushed to push a piece in my mouth, realised in time that it was heavily salted and spat it out, but many of the poor wretches ate it. And you know what! That day they gave us no water at all, so several of those who ate the fish were driven nearly insane with thirst. Then I saw a terrible thing in our truck. One man, going crazy I think, urinated into his cupped hands and drank the liquid. That poor fellow died later in agony".

I could not absorb the full horror, none of us could and seeing the shocked expressions on our faces, Mum said:

"Do you really want me to go on with this?"

"Yes", said John, "Unless it is too painful for you, but I think we should know what happened to you both in that accursed Siberia". I was very distressed for I never imagined for one moment that Mum had endured so much.

She continued after a sip of wine. "All I ask of you children is that after my death you give water for my soul. You do not have the slightest idea what thirst means. She paused and crossed herself.

"I thought this awful journey would never end. Whenever the doors opened now I noticed that the landscape was becoming more bleak and it was getting much colder. Then at one stop we were ordered out of the train. Poor us, we were so weak and stiff with the cramped conditions we could hardly move, but they forced us into a column once we set foot on the ground, and marched us along, helped by blows from the guard's rifles and some snarling dogs they had with them. At last we reached some barns where they shut us in. The earth floor was covered in straw and at least we had room to lie down. It was such a comfort to stretch my body. We all collapsed and lay where we fell, exhausted.

In that barn I think I saw the devil!" said Mum, unexpectedly changing the subject. We laughed at such a statement, with some relief at her change in tone. She continued, giving us a little smile. "By now it was quite dark, with just some pale moonlight filtering between the gaps in the boards. I made myself more comfortable by putting my quilt half underneath me and half over, to try to sleep. But the thoughts about you and your dad, and the worry over what was to happen to me kept me awake. As I lay there I suddenly heard a fluttering noise in the air. Because the sound was repeated a few times I strained my eyes to see what caused it. I distinguished in the gloom above me a dark shape like that of a bird, but with strange wings and the head of a mouse. Such an apparition I had never seen in my life so I thought it can't be anything else on this earth but the devil!

Quickly I pulled the cover over me to shut it out but under the quilt wrapped so tightly I could not breathe. I felt as though a heavy weight was pressing on me and, worried I would suffocate, I flung off the quilt, got to my knees and crossed myself several times. 'God banish this devil from me', I whispered. And what do you think, my dears, after I did so that devil vanished and no longer circled in the night to taunt me".

While relating this episode, funny for us, Mum was gesticulating and making the sign of the cross as she relived the experience. We just laughed until our sides ached.

"It wasn't any sort of devil, Mum", I said, "just a poor bat, a little animal which hides in the day in barns and comes out at night to hunt for food!"

"So, Lia, you do not think it was the devil?" asked Mum, beginning to smile as she watched us laughing so heartily. She then continued her harrowing story and our laughter died. "Next day we were marched back to the train and herded into the trucks to continue our journey. It was a gruelling struggle for us to survive against the torture of thirst, hunger and the cruelty of the guards in this dreadful journey which lasted so long. When we stepped from the cattle trucks at last, exhausted, bewildered and very frightened, they marched us into a prison at a place called Kansk, about three thousand miles from home! Of the original number of prisoners put in the truck with me, I think only a handful could have survived.

The prison we now entered was specially designed for *Kulaks* and so called 'Enemies of the People'. The cells were dark, with damp walls, and no heating. Plank shelves, one above the other unto the ceiling, served as beds. A blanket, so old as to be from the time of the Czar, was issued to each of us, and they were all infested with lice and bugs. For a toilet there was the usual half a small barrel, which added to the already awful stench. Food was disgusting and the only time we had any fresh air was when we were taken out, in batches of fifteen to twenty at a time, into a small dark yard with high walls, for exercise. I can't describe my feelings of desolation and hopelessness. It was only the thoughts of you and Theodore which gave me the will to stay alive.

After several months in this cold hell I was taken out with some others and again herded into one of the filthy cattle truck trains for another journey. This lasted only about five days and ended in a freezing, desolated and inhospitable region called Irkuts, in a concentration camp. The place was surrounded by a high barbed wire fence with watch towers at intervals manned by soldiers with guns. Vicious looking dogs patrolled the wire fence. In the centre of this settlement stood rows of bare wooden huts. We, the women, were separated from the men and then pushed into one of the huts where they forced us to strip naked for a 'check'. Such an embarrassment never happened before in my life, to stay nude in front of so many others, including some men, in a freezing hut. We were inspected for lice, then shaved under the arms and of pubic hair by men barbers, leering all the time at us and touching us as they pleased. It was absolutely dreadful. If a woman objected she was hit by a rifle butt. When the check was over another lot, who were prisoners but trustees, came to look and decided which group and which hut we would be in.

These huts varied from bad to worse. For the beginning I stayed in one with two layers of sleeping shelves, but later moved to one with three levels. Some of them had not even straw on the boards. One or two had the luxury of one weak electric light which often failed, but most were provided with an oil lamp. The only means of heating was a primitive wood burning stove which, allowed only to be kindled when we returned from work, never warmed the hut. The one crumb of comfort was being put in the same barrack with some women from Bessarabia so at least I could speak to them in the same language.

Work started the day after we arrived, for this was a labour camp. Every morning early they gave us a bread ration of about ten ounces, which had to last all day, then we had a roll call outside, in any kind of weather: torrential rain, snow or blizzards. We had to work sixteen hours a day, and on top of that was the march back and forth to the worksite. When going to work I had a sack over my back in which I always carried my precious quilt and what little else I possessed. I was loaded like a donkey but there was no choice, for anything left in the huts was stolen. Can you imagine what a sight I must have looked!"

"What did you work at, *Mama*?" asked Constantin.

"What didn't I work at in those horrible years. I don't think I can really remember all that I was forced to do. The most common was logging, for on this the devils could find jobs for everyone, young or old, sick or crippled. I am telling you this for I can well recall one particular winter of very deep snow, when the trustees gathered together all the men who were disabled, some with only one arm, things like that, as long as they could somehow walk, and forced them to tread down the snow to make a track to the forest. I guess it is hard for you to believe but even if the snow reached as high as my chest we were still forced through it to collect up branches and burn them. Because they were green and wet they only smouldered and gave out clouds of smoke so most of the time everyone choked and coughed".

I felt numbed by all the terrible things Mum was telling us. How could humans treat each other in such a diabolical way? I was very distressed as she continued. "It was heart breaking to look at some prisoners, for they were so thin and weak, yet forced to cut down huge trees with only handsaws and axes. Most of them had no experience of this kind of work because they were intellectuals or had only worked in offices. As they did not know how to fell trees many were injured or even killed. The dead were left in the snow and the injured received no treatment, so that very few survived.

Another cruel job was that in the quarries. With large hammers we had to break up stone, load the broken pieces on to barrows and push or drag them to the railway for use on the railbeds. Only God knows how many times I fainted doing such hard work. But the worst of the jobs for me and the one I hated most was at the creosote pits. Here we had to impregnate shingles with the stinking liquid and after a day there I felt as though my whole body was soaked in the stuff. Clothes, hair and skin stank from the creosote and wherever I went it stayed with me. Washing did not easily remove it, it was just awful.

Slightly better were the agricultural camps, but you had to be really ill, or know someone, or be plain cunning to get there. After months of stone breaking and the creosote pits together with the constant worry about you and *Tata* I became very ill. I kept crying a great deal at night, my heart started to give me pain and I thought I would shortly die. However, one day a doctor came, and although I had only picked up a little Russian I managed to tell him of my trouble and my children at home. He must have found I was really ill, for he recommended me for light work and I was shifted to Kemerova, to an agricultural camp. I felt a little better here doing work I knew about, but it was still no picnic as the targets we had to reach were enormous. 'Light work' was a joke.

With the guards watching us like hawks no one could eat any of the produce we picked or dug up and at the end of the day we were lined up and searched. But necessity is a good teacher and despite the checks I did steal the odd potato or carrot. I noticed that we were never searched below the knees, so I made a long tube like pocket from the linings of my jacket sleeves and fixed it in such a way that the bottom of it was just above my skirt hem. The pleats of the skirt hid it well and I could push a potato or carrot, or whatever I could find into the pocket. But only God knows how terrified I was when I had to pass the check in case they found anything on me. The thought was enought to make you ill, for if they caught you, they would beat you viciously and stop your food ration for days.

Just imagine my life in these concentration camps! After a hard days work I would crawl exhausted, as the others, back to the hut, which was cold, having been empty all day. Nothing pleasant awaited there. Often soaked with rain or snow I needed to dry whatever I was dressed in, but in the cold winter if anyone took off her clothes she could literally freeze to death inside the hut, so usually I kept mine on and they dried on my body.

The food was so terrible our pigs would have refused it, and was much too little to appease the pangs of hunger. In a huge pot of boiling water they dropped in some dirty unpeeled potatoes, and this was the best soup! Otherwise black cabbage, beetroot leaves, bran and all sorts of trash went into the cauldron. Some days we got just an unsalted infusion of nettles and a thin gruel of oats and barley. A camp I cannot forget (for we were moved from camp to camp depending on the work) was the one with a shortage of water. Here we got only a plate of gruel a day and two cups of brackish water, tasting of salt. My God how much I suffered in that place from thirst!

I suppose supplies of some proper food were sent to the camps, but if so the camp authorities and trustees stole it all. Nothing decent ever reached the prisoners. We were really starving at the time and would eat anything; leaves, herbs, wild berries, otherwise I am sure we would have died from malnutrition and starvation.

After years in a camp people lost all human ideals and became like animals, only survival counted. Consequently you could trust no one at all. When I stole a potato or a carrot I had to find a corner to hide and eat it raw so that no one would see me. What an existence!"

Mum paused, her face strained, mopped her brow and took some deep breaths, looking quite tired after the effort and emotion of recalling her suffering. Dad put his arm around her shoulders and said, tenderly, "You rest a while, Nicola, it's my turn to say a few words, but let us have another glass of wine and drink to our good health now that we are all here!" Dad then continued. "For me it was much the same. I stayed first in the prison in Orhei, then moved to Kishnev, from where I was sent, on exactly the same sort of train journey Mum has told you about, to a prison at Tomsk, then on again to a labour camp at Komsomolsk, almost to Japan.

Once there I did my share of logging, and worked in the mines for coal and copper. Many a time I've stood all day long up to the waist in water digging peat from a bog or cutting grass from the hummocks in a swamp. I suppose for me the logging was the least of all the evils.

I tried hard to look upon any work as a job to be done and not hate it. In this way I often exceeded the norm, for which I was given extra food. I had the advantage that I was used to hard work and enjoyed doing it. However the prisoners who hated the work and did not reach their targets had their food rations cut, many dying from starvation. Then we had the extra work of digging in the frozen ground to bury them. That was like breaking concrete with picks and shovels.

From time to time we were checked for our ability to work as most of us looked like shadows. How do you think they checked us? Well, I'll tell you. They made us strip and bend over, then decided by how much flesh we had on our buttocks. If your bones stuck out, with no flesh on them, you were considered unfit for work".

"What happened to the unfit ones?" asked Basil.

"I don't really know, they were just marched off and we never saw them again, but I can tell you what happened to me once at a new camp when I was found unfit, for I looked like a skeleton. They sent me to queue up in front of a certain hut for a bath. In any civilised place I would have welcomed this, for I could not remember when I last had a proper wash. But now I thought if I take my clothes off here, in this dreadful camp, someone will steal my sheepskin jacket, the only thing I have to stop me freezing. Determined to not lose that, I just waited my chance, and when the trustees attention was diverted by some argument further down the queue, seeing it was all pretty chaotic, I slipped along the side of the hut and joined the 'fit' group, who were not lined for a bath. To my stupefaction I heard later that there were no baths, the people in the queue were killed in that hut by being gassed.

"Who told you such a horrific thing, Dad?" asked Sanda.

"One of the prisoners who was sent to clear out the bodies. He also told me of a woman who survived the gassing almost by a miracle, for she fell down near a hole in the hut side and had enough air to breathe to keep her alive. They took her out with the dead and let her get away. God knows what happened to her afterwards".

"I thought only the Germans gassed people, now you are saying the Russians did it as well?" queried Basil, unbelievingly.

"Yes, they did. Is it so surprising? They shot people, beat them to death, killed them in Siberia by starvation and slavery, why shouldn't they gas people as well?"

"It sounds as though that sheepskin jacket saved your life", said John.

"Or God did, for I was saved from death by some miracle four times in all. The first time in Kishnev. After they took me in 1940, there was that earthquake. Well, much of the prison building collapsed and many were killed, but my section stayed up."

"I remember the earthquake" I interrupted, "I was playing in the yard when suddenly the chickens began to run about as though in panic. The other animals started to make a tremendous din. Then the ground moved under me as though I was standing on jelly. Straw fell from the stacked sheaves and the tools rattled in their racks. I was frightened and ran into Mum. Then we heard later that some buildings in Kishnev had been damaged".

"Well, one of those was the prison", continued Dad, and, as I have just said, the second time was the gassing".

"And what was the third time, for I suppose the fourth was here when you were looking after the calves?" "You're right . . . the third time? Oh yes, that happened when I was in Khabarovsk, another logging camp. We had to cut down trees and haul them to the river with ropes as though we were horses or oxen. We floated them in the water and had to tie them in crude rafts to drift downstream. But because the logs often jammed on their way, the trustees ordered someone to ride on each raft to clear the jams. It was very dangerous work, but they always seemed to pick the weakest looking men to go. I think it was deliberate, one way of getting rid of the feeble, for if you fell in the river, and many did, you had little chance to survive.

Anyhow, I was picked once to ride one of these batches of logs and found myself washed off into the water. I couldn't swim, but again a miracle happened, for as I hit the water my sheepskin jacket spread out like two wings and somehow kept me afloat enough to reach one side of the river. In desperation I grabbed at some tree roots and struggled out bit by bit until I collapsed on the bank".

"Couldn't you have then escaped?" asked Sanda naively.

"Escaped! Where on earth to go, my girl, in that vast wilderness, with the forest which seems to stretch for ever? I had no food, no money, no papers and not much strength. Moreover, I did not know exactly where I was, and there were wolves and bears roaming the forest. Anyway, the guards with their dogs would soon have caught me. No, I never gave it a thought, I just prayed so thankfully that the Good Lord had saved me again. There was also an incident which stopped me even dreaming of any attempt to escape. One night two prisoners crawled under the wire and ran away. They must have been courageous or foolish, or very desperate, or all three, I don't know. What I do know is that in a very short time they were caught and brought back, beaten in front of us all until they were bleeding and senseless then the dogs were set on them.

They were always beating someone in the camps. If you were struggling to push a barrow loaded with stone and, being so weak, collapsed, they would come over and kick you or hit you with their rifle butts until you dragged yourself upright and continued working. One day, coming back from diggng tunnels, a prisoner stepped out of line to pick up a cigarette butt a guard had thrown down. Immediately a dog was set on him and he was beaten back into the column. He had to be supported by others all the way back to the camp. There was no regard for life at all. So many died in rockfalls and other stupid accidents, for there was no concept of safety".

"Oh, Dad, it's awful and unbelievable what you are telling us!" I said, holding his hand.

"My dear Lia", interrupted Mum, "that's nothing compared with the number who died of cold, hunger and disease. Because of so many deaths I sometimes had to play the role of priest. It happened for the first time when a pretty young woman from Bessarabia died in our hut. My conscience just would not allow me to see her thrown in a hole without a word said, like a dead dog, and as we stood around this grave I suddenly found myself praying and singing hymns that I remembered from the burial service at home:

> *"I looked in a grave and saw only the bare bones,*
> *This life is but a shadow and a dream,*
> *The dream fades away,*
> *The shadow disappears,*
> *This life is as nothing".*

Then, when I started to sing another part of the service the women from Bessarabia joined me. This was such an uplifting moment, all felt closer to each other. In the evenings, when they were lying exhausted on the planks, I would sometimes sing hymns for them and tell stories of the saints. It helped me to forget the misery for a little while, and I also felt that the other women respected me as I seemed to raise their morale. As you know, I have always had great faith in God and I think in Siberia this helped me greatly to survive.

When anyone died there was usually a fight between the prisoners as to who had what of the dead persons's clothing, for everything was so scarce. It meant that most times the dead were buried completely naked. After a few years work in Siberia we were dressed much worse than beggars! When we arrived some of us had decent clothes, but as you very well know, nothing lasts for ever. Boots and shoes were torn to pieces on the rocky ground. Sleeves of jackets pulled out and elbows developed holes. Jackets and trousers or skirts were ripped and torn with carrying branches or forcing our way through the forest. We ended by wearing jackets with the fronts, sleeves and backs each of a different colour, some with so many patches you could not tell what was the original material. Later, when we were allowed to receive parcels, the sacking in which they were wrapped was all used to patch clothes and many of us walked about with names and addresses still visible on our rags. I suppose I could laugh now, but at the time it was a heartbreaking sight.

I myself had no choice but to make some boots, using pieces of old torn up padded jackets for the uppers and layers of felt and rubber tyre for the soles, so that I could fight the cold in that accursed Siberia, for there was snow lying about most of the time, and often the temperature dropped to sixty below zero. Blizzards were everlasting raging in the winter, and all liquids froze solid. Even when the weather softened it was still bad, for then we had slushy snow and rain, and the very cold winds."

"What was it like in Summer?" asked Mary.

"A little better for it was sometimes warm but so short a season! Still, in spite of the milder weather I could not enjoy it much for there were hordes of these horrible horse flies, which stung any uncovered flesh, bringing up huge swellings. They were an awful pest, getting in everywhere; sleeves, necks, hair and even under skirts.

But now you have had enough of my story. I'd better go and do some cooking. Your father will tell you more if you still want to hear". We did want to hear, so Dad continued with his side of the tragedy.

"Well, as I've said, I worked in the mines and quarries, in swamps and on the railway, but most of the time on logging. It was backbreaking work for prisoners as weak and ill as we were.

In winter the terrible cold and short daylight made it impossible to work outside for long, so they cut our rations dramatically. On one of these days, while stuck in the camp, I saw a frail looking woman, who worked in the canteen for the bosses, trying to chop logs. I felt sorry for her and went to help cut and carry the wood. She was so moved by my gesture tears came to her eyes. So, whenever I could I chopped wood for the canteen. In this way I became known to the women working there and from time to time they took the risk of slipping me some crusts of bread, or whatever they could, and that helped me to survive.

After I had done about six years, still on logging, a guard called me over. I wondered what I had done wrong and expected a beating, but instead he said.

"You seem to work hard and say little, I've an extra job for you. The commandant needs some work done at his house, I'll take you there. I followed him to the house, some distance away from the camp. It was quite a large Dacha with a big yard, and here the guard left me with the commandant, who said.

"I want you to do some jobs about the house, like cutting wood and fetching water, keeping the yard clean and anything else my wife demands. To do this you'll come here Sundays instead of going to the forest". I was quite pleased for this break, for no work about the house could be as hard as logging.

The commandant's wife was a pale delicate creature who had three children, one a baby. I felt some pity for her, for somehow she was as much a prisoner of Siberia as I, so I struggled to do my best, keeping the wood store filled and the water butts topped up, cleaning out the animals and the yard. Having learned some Russian at school gave me an advantage for I was able to communicate with the wife and tell her of my six children at home, and that I had committed no crime other than that of being a *Kulak*. As she became aware that I was honest and did all she asked of me, she began to give me some food, which added to the camp ration.

After about a year of this extra work at the house, the commandant said, quite unexpectedly, that he would give me a paper stating my sentence was finished. I thought he was joking with me, and felt bitter that he should play with me like this, for I could not believe him. But a few days later he did hand me the document and said. "You're free now, you can leave the camp!"

I was so overcome by this gesture I did not know what to do and found myself kneeling in front of him and kissing his hands. With tears in my eyes and an overwhelming happiness in my heart I took the paper and hurried back to the camp to collect anything I had and quickly get out of the place before anyone could change their minds. But this exultation did not last long, for as I walked free through the gates a frightening question came to me. How was I to get home without money or food? I felt suddenly completely disorientated and lost, but decided in the end to hang around until one of the camp supply lorries came by and I could beg a lift to some populated place in this wilderness, where I could find some work in order to get money for the rail fare home. From that day I worked anywhere, on the roads or collectives, as long as I earned something, hitching lifts from place to place. As I wanted to save everything for the fare home, I could never pay for any lodging but stayed in barns or stables, or wherever shelter was free.

Believe me or not it took a year of this sort of hard life to save enough roubles for the ticket. When, at last, I thought I had sufficient money, I set out for the station at Khabarovsk. There, to my utter consternation, the ticket clerk said. "I can't accept these old roubles, go to the bank and change them for new ones". At the bank I found the rouble had been devalued and in exchange I received only enough new roubles to take me less than half way home. I was so shocked and upset I thought I might as well be dead, for it seemed I would never get away from that God forsaken place. Oh, Dear Lord, I prayed, what can I do now? How much longer have I got to endure this sort of existence to earn the extra roubles? I must start to slave again, what other choice have I?

I cannot remember with any certainty how long it took me to get enough money for that elusive ticket, but it was at least another year. What I do remember is that that hand to mouth life was almost as bad as being in the camps.

Eventually and almost unbelievably I did board the train. The tears ran down my face as I crossed myself and thanked God for keeping me alive all those years, to finally reach the glorious day when I could go home. The journey back was still very long, but at least in proper coaches, not in a cattle truck. Moreover, the fact that I was on my way to Slobozia gave me strength. While sitting in the train my thoughts drifted back to the earlier years, visions of ploughing the fields with the two horses, myself between the plough shafts and George or Ephraim leading the animals. All day long we would plod the length of the field, turning the dead stubble into dark furrowed stripes, until, as the sun was dying in the sky, the whole land would look as rich dark corduroy. The birds would be out gathering tasty meals from the newly turned earth. Then there was the rolling and harrowing to break the clods and clean the weeds, which had to be gathered and burnt, scenting the air with an odour which foretold the coming of spring. I thought of the sowing which followed and the never ending round of hoeing that Nicola had shared in the past years. All of you sons of mine came to my vision. George and Ephraim who had helped on the farm, and you three, who were just at the age to give a hand with the extra land, when all finished with my deportation. . . I couldn't stop the tears coming as the train crossed the Dnistru into my beloved Bessarabia, which I had not seen for eight years".

"But, Dad, how did Mum get home?" asked Basil. "She didn't say anything about working for her fare?"

"No, she had nothing like that to do. When she had finished her seven years (and, like me, she was supposed to be sentenced to five), being quite ill they gave her a travel pass. For her it was still a hellish journey, lasting several days, in which the only food she had was given to her by some other passengers, for she had no money at all."

I thought my parent's story was such a powerful and moving account of two innocent people working and surviving in the most horribly inhumane conditions imagineable. Before this reunion I had no idea how much cruelty and degredation they had suffered and I felt stunned and sickened by their revelations.

Mum came to tell us it was time for lunch and it was later in the afternoon before Dad resumed the second part of his saga.

"It is impossible now to describe my feelings as I approached Kiperceni and the places once so familiar to me. So many changes in the look of the fields upset me greatly, for all the beautiful coloured strips of different vegetables and cereals formerly belonging to the private farms had now been replaced by unending stretches of tobacco and maize. I felt excited, yet very nervous as to what I would find in Slobozia.

In the bus, on the last stage of my journey, I looked unseeingly through the dirt caked windows, thinking about the green village of my youth, listening to the nearby snatches of conversation in my sweet Moldavian, not the hated Russian, until my thoughts were brought back to the present by the jolting and screeching of the vehicle as it ground to a halt. I stepped from the bus, my feet hurrying to the village, anxious to know if there was any news of Nicola, eternally in my thoughts and prayers, as you all were. I heard from George, after years of deportation, when letters were permitted, that Nicola had also been deported, a year after me. I thanked God to know you children had escaped to Romania. As our house, land and goods had all been confiscated I had no choice but to ask to stay for a while with George and Marika.

Imagine my feelings, if you can, when I opened the gate and saw Nicola standing by the well. For a moment I thought I was hallucinating, it was so unbelievable. We rushed into each others arms, holding tightly together, both crying and not speaking, staying clasped in that embrace until we heard Marika calling.

"George, George, come quickly to see this miracle, your father is home!" Then their children, Anouska and Boris came out to see. At first I couldn't recognise them, they had only been tots when I was taken.

'This is your *Bunicu*, come and give him a kiss!' But the children were shy and embarrassed, not remembering me. 'Oh, you are so big now, and I am too weak to carry you in my arms as I used to when you were tiny'.

Then we had a little celebration, but there was not much to celebrate with. After all the hungry times I had been through, I came back and found terrible shortages in my own village, for the previous year there had been such a prolonged drought that the crops had failed. Hardly enough cereals had been grown to provide the next years seed corn. There was also a plague of rats which made it worse as they spoiled so much".

Ileana, who had joined us and listened to Dad, now said. "Leave me to tell them about that, father, I know better, I was here all the time". She then continued while Dad sighed deeply and thankfully rested.

"Everybody in the village tried to ration themselves and keep something in reserve, but this was almost impossible for the central government still demanded its normal quotas from the collectives. People buried grain and supplies to try and hide them, but spies were sent out to look for any newly turned earth and dig it over. If they did find anything then the owner was deported. We were all really desperate, eating leaves from trees, dandelions and weeds, anything. It's hard to believe now but some people ground up even oak bark to mix with any proper flour they had. If anyone succeeded in hiding some grain, of course he could not take it to the mill, so had to grind it by hand with two stones, like in the middle ages. Your Auntie Alexandra's husband, Uncle Vasile, died from malnutrition, his stomach swelling up like a balloon and people said that was from the oak bark".

I felt deeply sorry for my poor parents, to come home from Siberia and be inundated with such bad news in their own village. Ileana continued "It was all caused by this stupid collectivisation, for when the Russians came back in 1944 they stole everything from us: land, animals, crops. Then they forced us to plant new things, like this tobacco, which reduced the area for food crops. So the next year there was very little to harvest. That's how long the shortages had been going on. The collectives were then and still are useless. Everyone has to work in them for next to nothing. Each day some hours are wasted while one brigadier or other decides who does what. You only need to be in the fields hoeing and see all the slackers just about moving their arms, to feel like giving them a good dig with a pitchfork. In spite of that, when you go for your dole, you find they get more than you because they are friends or relatives of some official or other who has fiddled the books."

After she had finished her outburst Dad took up the thread again. "We started soon to work in the collective, for it was not fair for Marika to feed Nicola and me as well as giving us shelter. It took some time to get used to the new way of life and of working in the village, but we managed to do so and were able to pay for our keep. But just as we thought ourselves settled in the frightening rumour came about more families being sent to Siberia. Stalin had decided to fully develop that region and to get the necessary labour force he decreed that a percentage of each village population be sent to that accursed land. Mum and I thought ourselves safe because we had already been there, but we were wrong. The local authorities made a list of families to go, yet some of these had been warned somehow and had gone into hiding. These evil authorities, determined to make up the number, arrested us again, less than one year after our release. We were terribly shocked and tried to protest but no one took any notice, just forced us back into that hell.

This time we ended up at Barnaul, in the Altaisk region, not so far as previously. We were not imprisoned but forced to work in an agricultural camp. Being together made it a little easier than before, and we had no need to worry so much about you as we knew you were safe in Romania, although we had no idea where. In this camp, after some months of hard labour, we were given a small hut to ourselves, a tiny share of the crops and some dole, and by working longer hours and saving every penny we managed to buy a cow.

In 1953, as you know very well, the great tyrant died. While millions were mourning him we joyfully thanked God for ridding us of this bloodthirsty evil monster Stalin. Once Khruschev came to power everyone began to feel as though the chains were broken, yet the changes were tantalisingly slow and it took another four years for us to be granted freedom to return home.

When the marvellous day came we sold all we possessed there in order to afford the train fares to Slobozia. Back in the village we went again to George and Marika's house, but to our astonishment strangers were living there now. We found that after we had been taken to Siberia for the second time George thought that he and Marika might be caught in the net, so they abandoned everything and ran away to escape, as Ephraim already told you.

What to do now? We had no place to go anymore! I went to see the president of the Colhoz, but he said sarcastically "There are no empty houses in the village for *Kulaks*, you'd better go and see what your son can do for you!" Ephraim emptied this old house, which he had been using as a store, and helped us to make it liveable. We had absolutely nothing in the beginning and had to ask Ileana to lend us everything, even to a knife and spoon" Father finished his story with a sigh of relief.

"My heart aches each time I look back and see how we were forced to abandon you when so young and left you wandering about the world lacking everything, especially our love. We must have sinned badly before God that he punished us so harshly". So saying Mum prayed aloud. "We thank you dear God for giving us the chance to be together again, parents and children". Then she rose to her feet and said. "But let us forget that terrible past and be happy now we have reached these wonderful days when we are all here. It is one of the most magnificent moments in my life, for I never dreamed that after nearly two decades of separation we should ever see each other again. I can't tell you how proud I am of the way you have all struggled to make careers far beyond my wildest dreams. My three sons all doctors, two of my daughters teachers and one an editor! You have done better than the children of some rich families. With such fine jobs I am sure you will have marvellous futures and enjoy your lives".

During the days we spent together I could see my parents gaining strength and becoming more like the Mum and Dad I once knew. Some laughter crept into their voices, Mum began to smile more often and even sing again while she was cooking the wonderful meals I remembered of old. I now happily began to feel they were the beloved parents I had longed for so much and not the strangers I had encountered that first day. The time spent there in our reunion was magnificent, and every dream came true when George and Marika made the journey from their village to visit us, and the whole family was together once more in Slobozia.

George and Marika arrived to a welcome of tears, laughter and long, long embraces. To my eyes they were only a little older, but still as full of warmth and kindness as I remembered.

"It's incredible! Are you the kids I had to chase each morning to get things done? Look at the boys, George, they are now taller than you", said Marika in wonder.

I wanted to know how they fared, abandoning all they had and leaving our village. George was pleased to tell me.

"I wasn't going to sit about here and be sneered at by these louts for being the son of a *Kulak*, so we left everything and chanced it. It wasn't that easy for in any nearby village someone, sooner or later, recognised me and we had to move on, being scared all the time of being caught for deportation, but eventually we ended at Corneşti, and that was far enough away. The collective gave us an old broken down house, but it had a large garden and then God favoured us, for I won enough money on the state lottery to help build a new house. As I knew about bees from Dad, I soon took the job of looking after the collectives hives, which suited me. Naturally the honey belonged to the Colhoz, but I still had enough for myself."

"Yet I heard you were a teacher for some time?"

"Oh, yes, that's a laugh. At school I had done a year longer than most, so being almost an intellectual I was chosen to do a six month's course, which made me a full blown teacher! Anyhow, we both worked hard, and I think if you do that, you can get most of what you want in life."

Alas, the time we had to spend with our parents came to an end. As we left, Mum and Dad stood by the gate, two small forlorn figures. I was filled with such sadness at parting with them again. Mum had hugged us tightly and said. "You will write us often, won't you. We shall live for your letters and please do come to see us whenever you can, for God knows how much longer we shall live".

From then on we tried to lighten their days and make them believe that life was still worth living, by writing frequently and planning to visit them as often as we could. Sadly Mum died from her heart trouble at the age of sixty four, following our second visit. It was so unfair that her life should end so soon after returning home from Siberia and being reunited with us.

Left alone Dad agreed to come to Romania and live with us. In spite of his terrible years in Siberia, he kept his health and lived to celebrate his ninety third anniversary.

My parents were martyrs to and victims of an ideology which they could never have foreseen would collapse and now be almost dead. I can only hope that in some way the successful lives that the six of us carved out for ourselves, with careers far above the highest they could dream, has been some compensation for Mum's and Dad's years of unspeakable suffering and helped to brighten their latter days.

At times I wonder what would have happened to me and my family if the Russians had never occupied Bessarabia. Would I have married one of Mum's favoured priests? Would I have become the wife of a farmer and still be living on a farm in that region? There can be no answer to this speculation.

I happily continued working as an editor in Bucharest until one day, when strolling in the beautiful Herastrau Park, I met a man who changed my life completely.

"Excuse me," asked the stranger, "do you speak English?"

"A little".

"Can you tell me where the Folk Museum is?"

Knowing some of the language from a three month intensive course I had just finished, I was quite pleased to show him the museum and make a tour of it so that I could practise what I had been taught. I never dreamed for a moment that this quiet and gentle Englishman would become my husband, but I certainly liked him right away. He took my address and wrote to me. From this beginning our romance blossomed with many letters and phone calls, later with Bill flying out quite often to see me until one Easter he asked me to marry him.

We spent a few wonderful holidays together in Romania during the two years of waiting for the authorities to grant permission for our marriage, which eventually took place on a Christmas Day. Since then I have lived with my husband a quiet and peaceful life in the beautiful county of Shropshire. We return often in summer to see my large family, enjoying being together in a pretty part of Romania where they all now live.